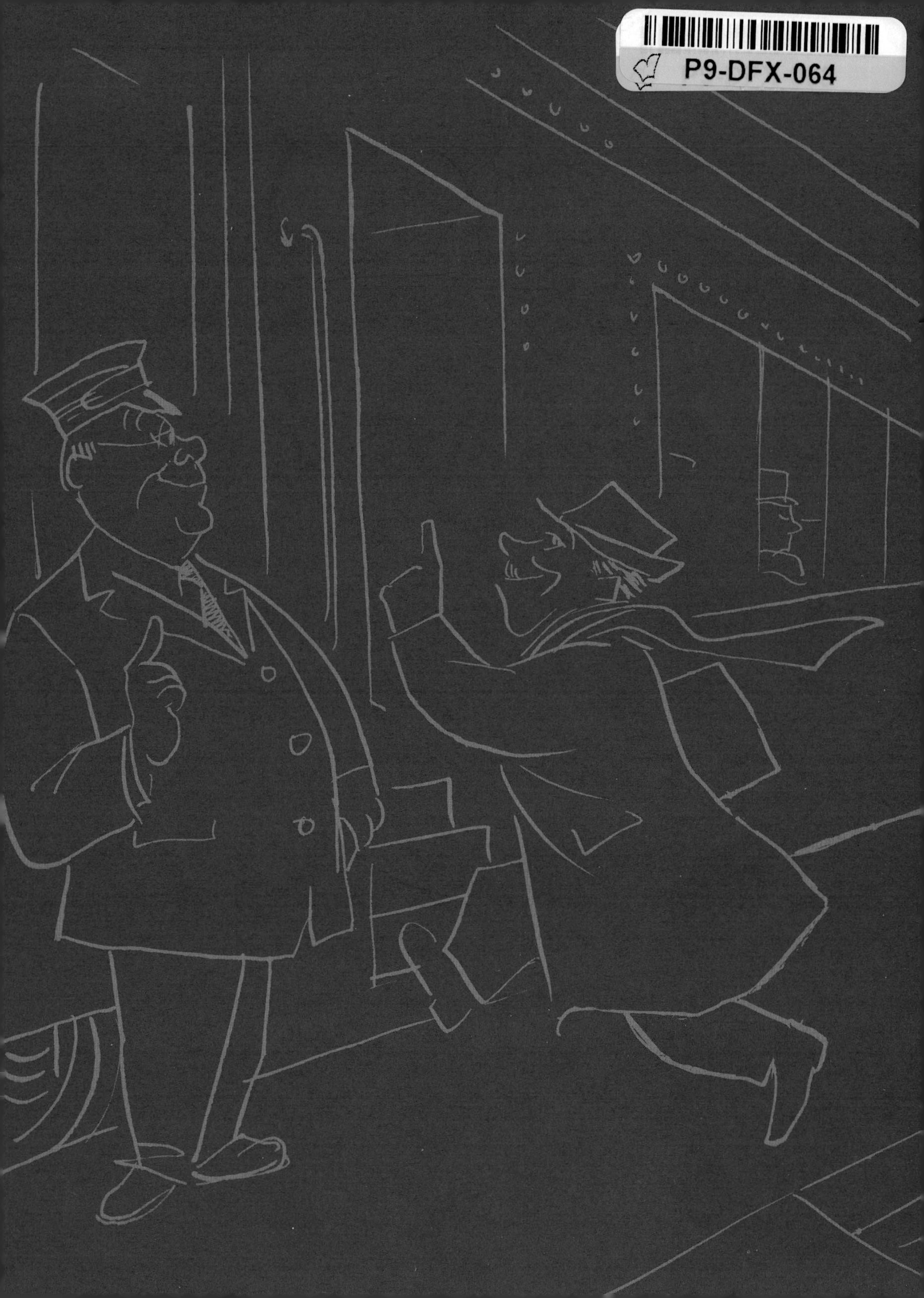

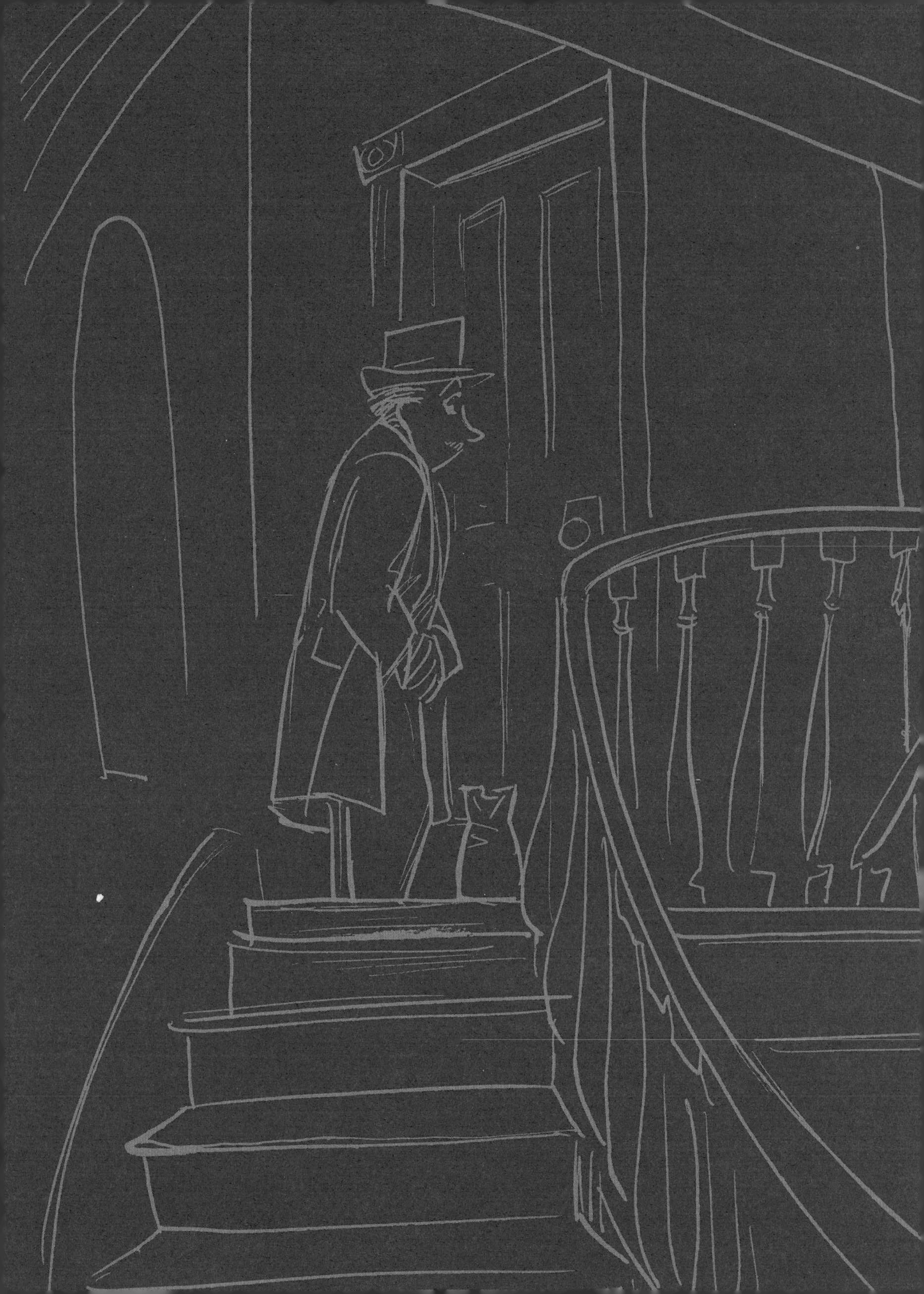

SKITZY

by
Don Freeman

THE STORY OF FLOYD W. SKITZAFROID

SKITZY

 Drawn & Quarterly Post; Office Box 48056, Montreal, Quebec Canada H2V 4S8; www.drawnandquarterly.com; First Hardcover edition: November 2008.; Printed in Canada.; ISBN 1-897299-58-6; 10 9 8 7 6 5 4 3 2 1; Library and Archives Canada Cataloguing in Publication; Freeman, Don, 1908-1978; Skitzy / Don Freeman.; ISBN 978-1-897299-58-6 (bound); I. Title.; PN6727.F713S55 2008 741.5'973 C2008-901256-9; Distributed in the USA and abroad by Farrar, Straus and Giroux; 19 Union Square West, New York, NY 10003; Orders: 888.330.8477; Distributed in Canada by Raincoast Books; 9050 Shaughnessy Street, Vancouver, BC V6P 6E5; Orders: 800.663.5714; For more information on Don Freeman, please visit www.donfreeman.info

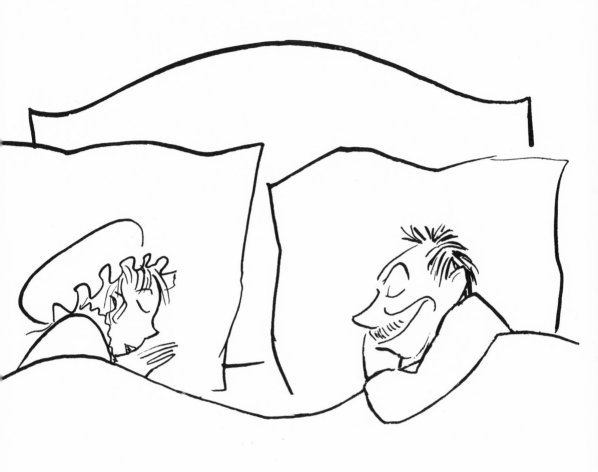

AS WE LOOK IN ON MR AND MRS SKITZAFROID
THEY APPEAR TO BE BLISSFULLY SLEEPING

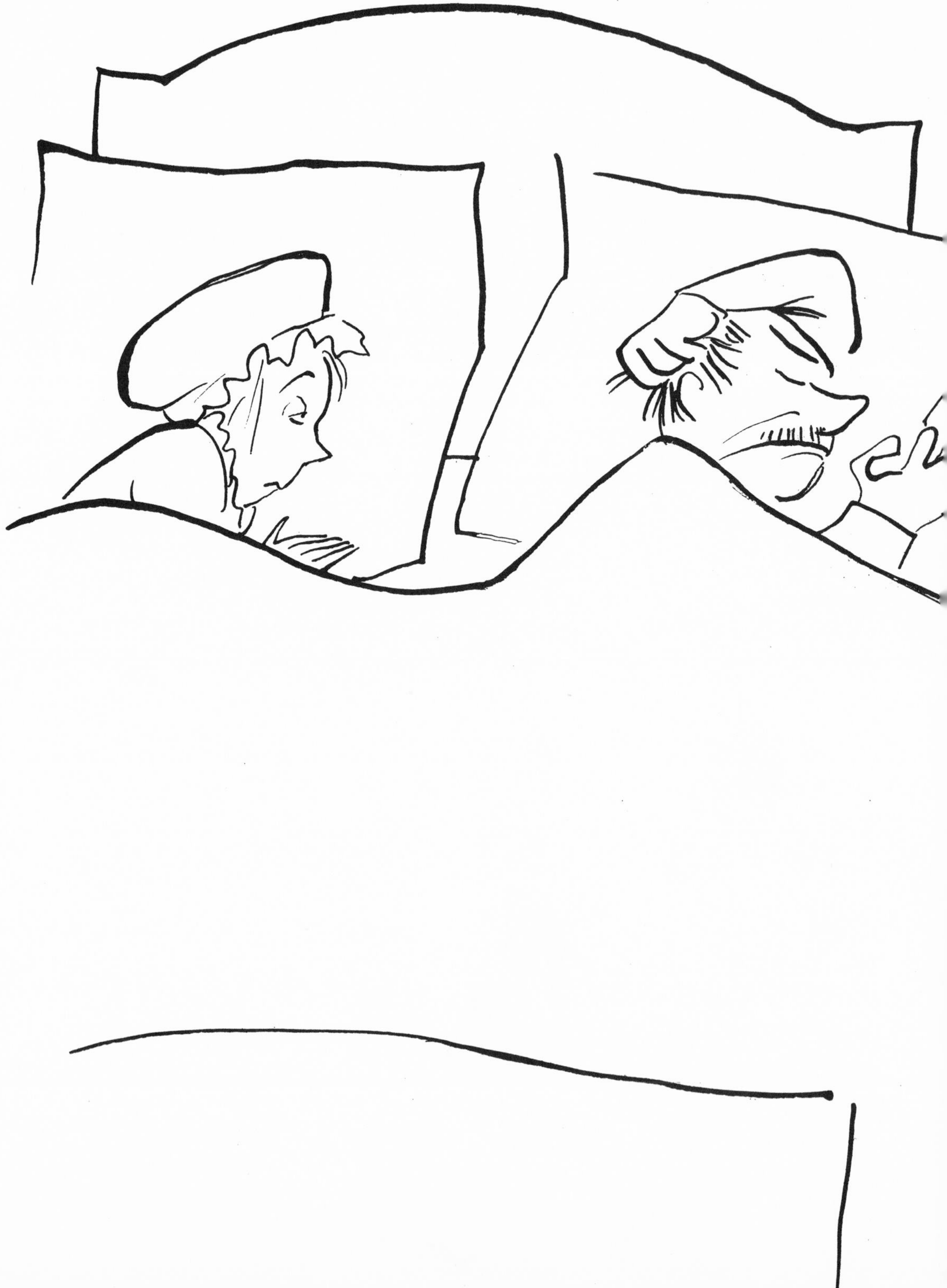

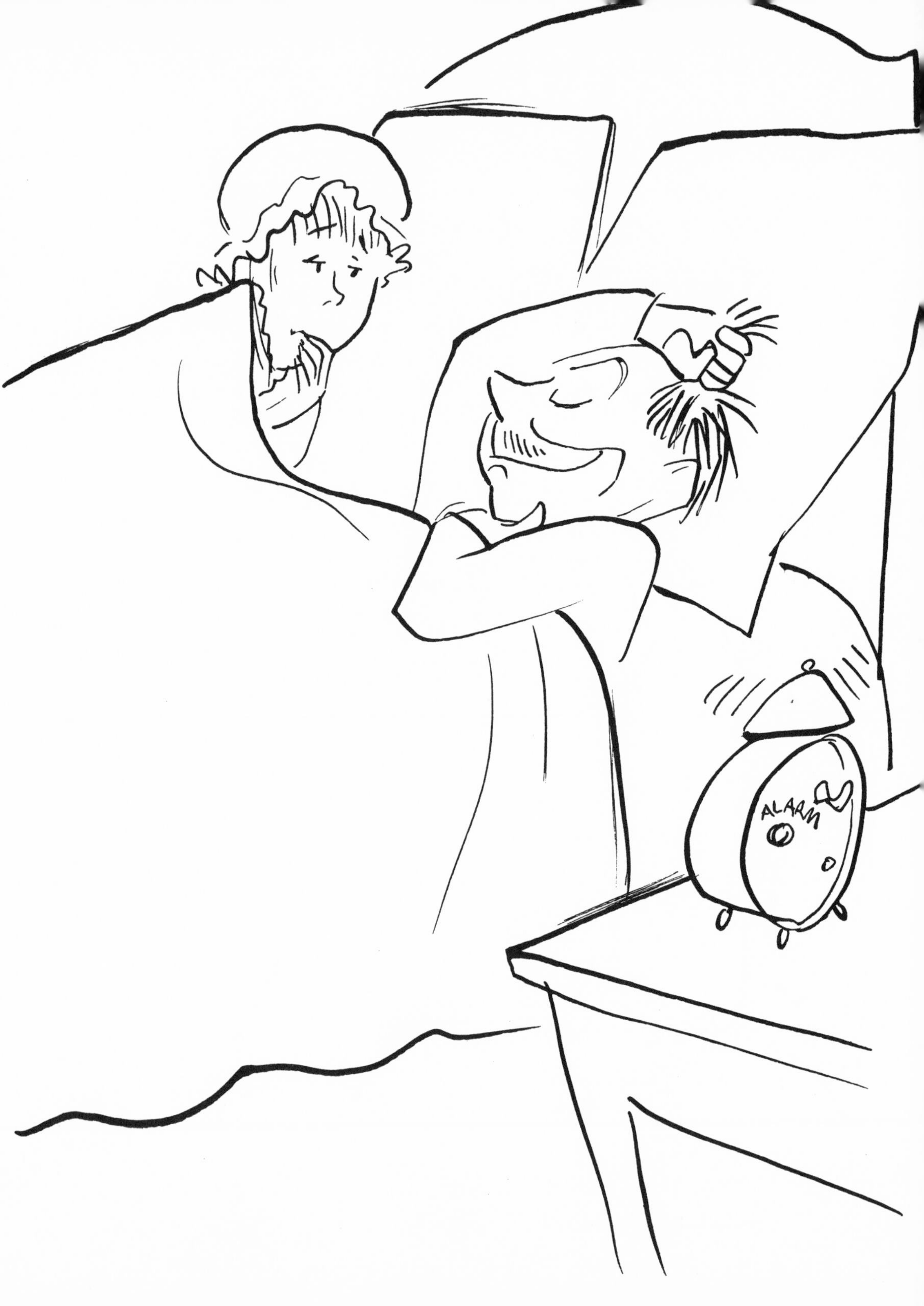
ALARM

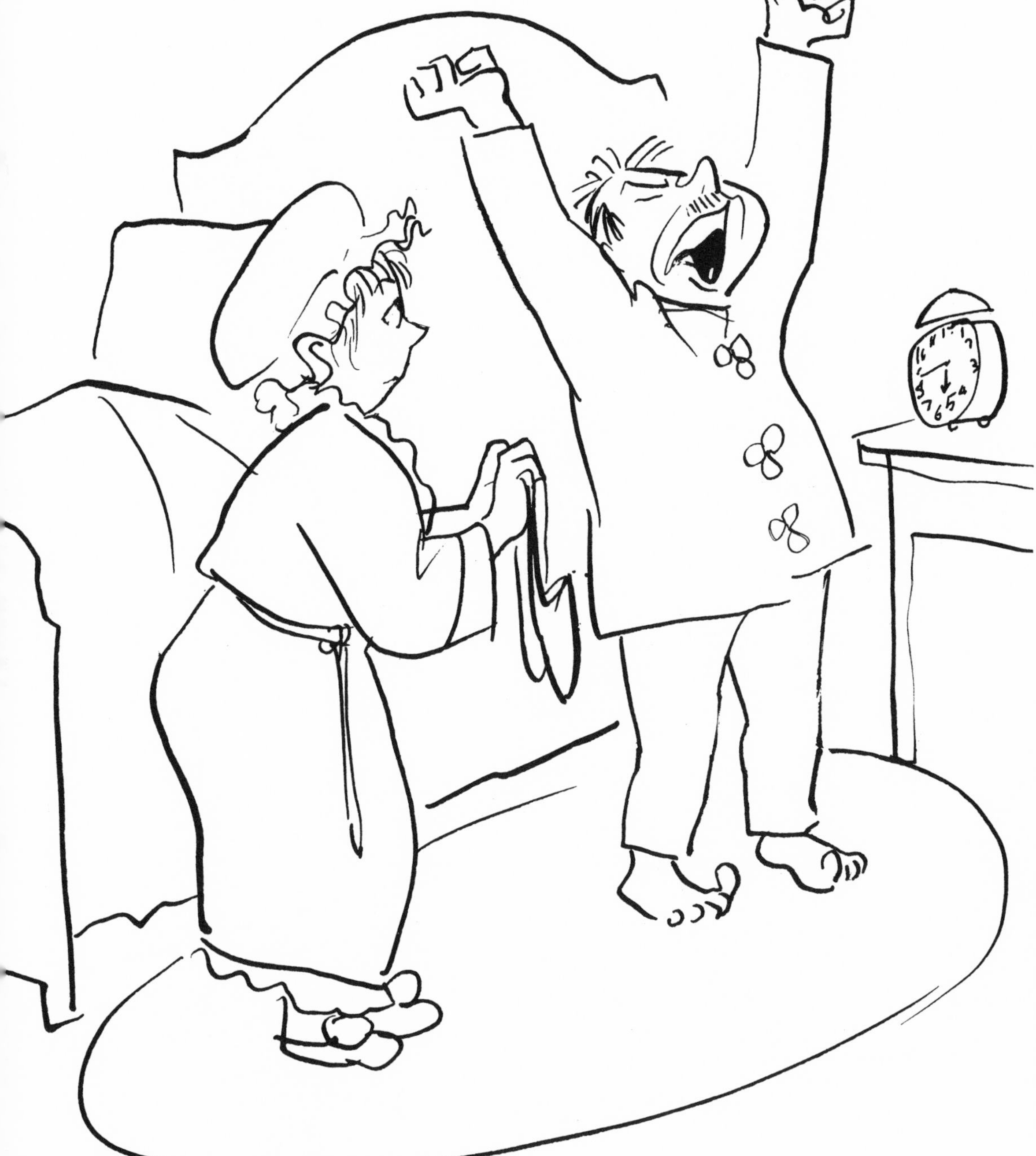

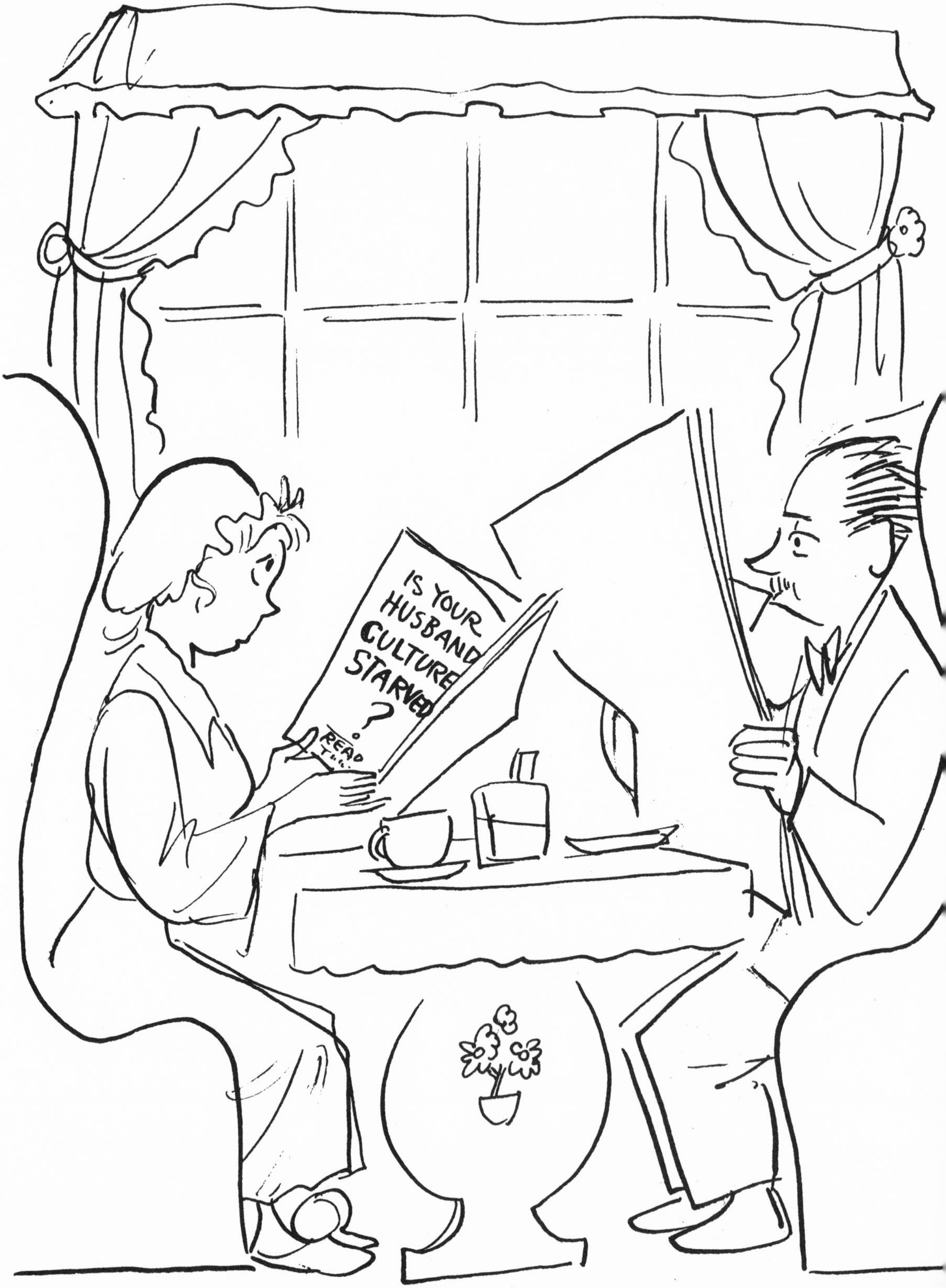
IS YOUR HUSBAND CULTURE STARVED ?
READ

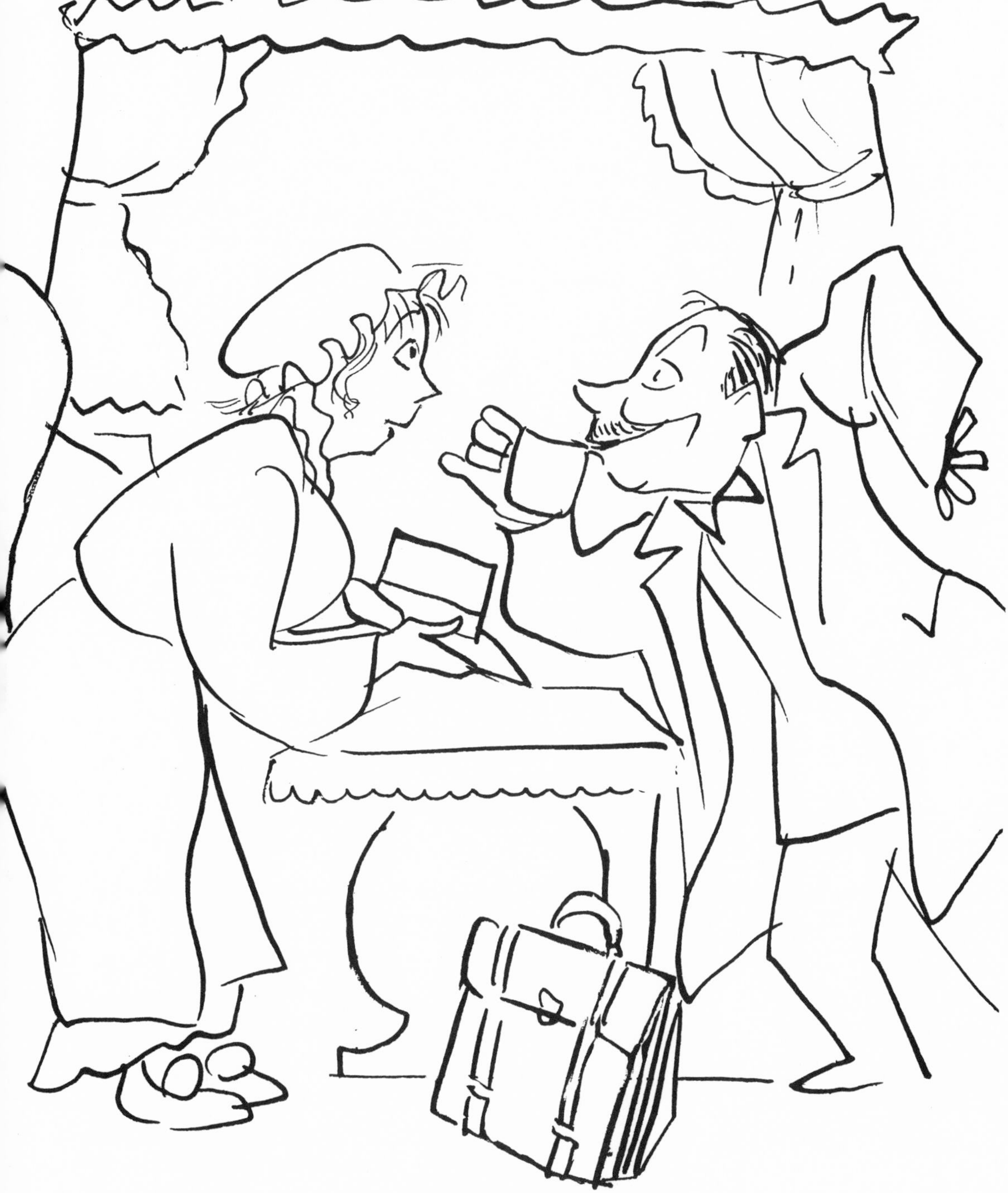

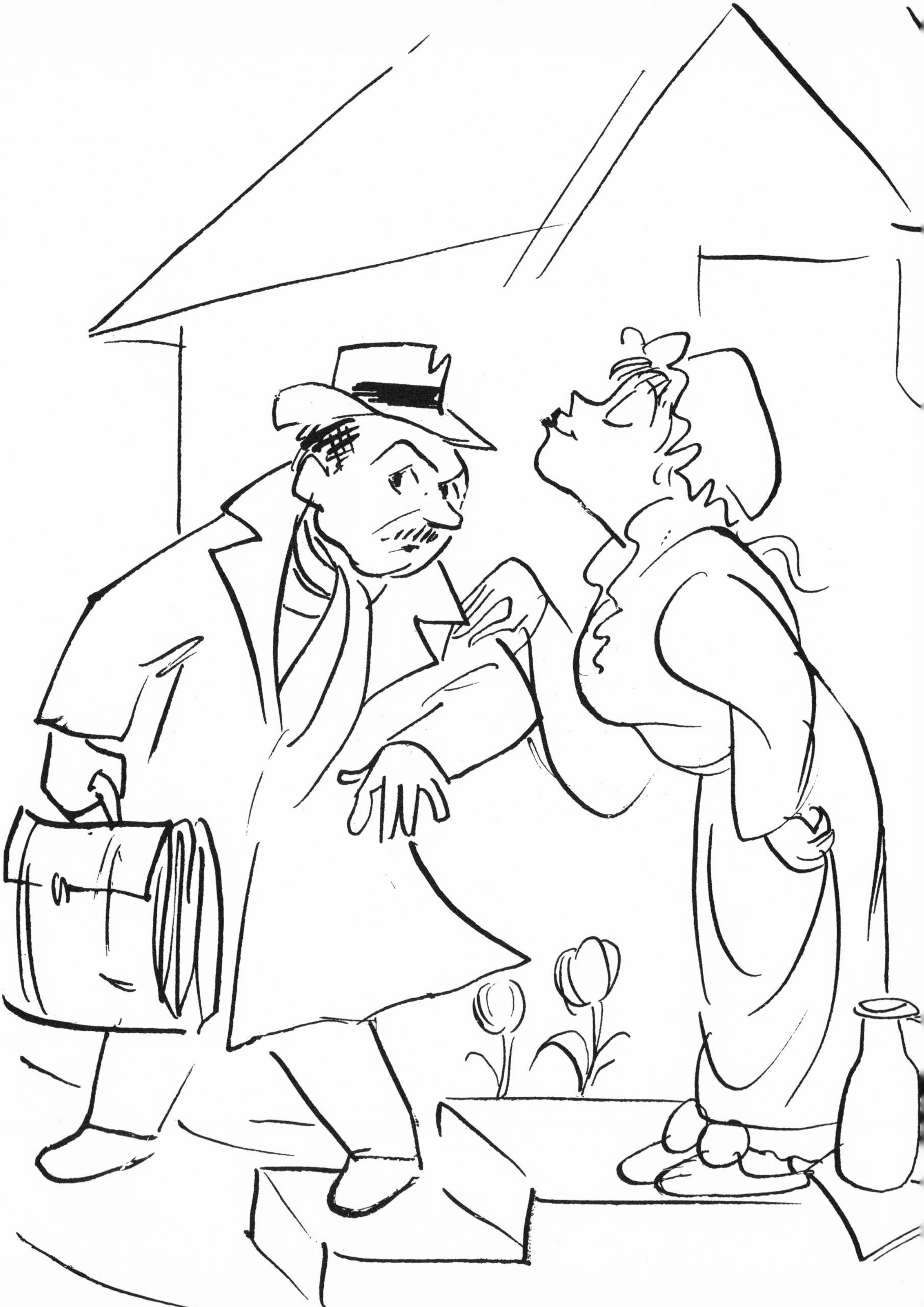

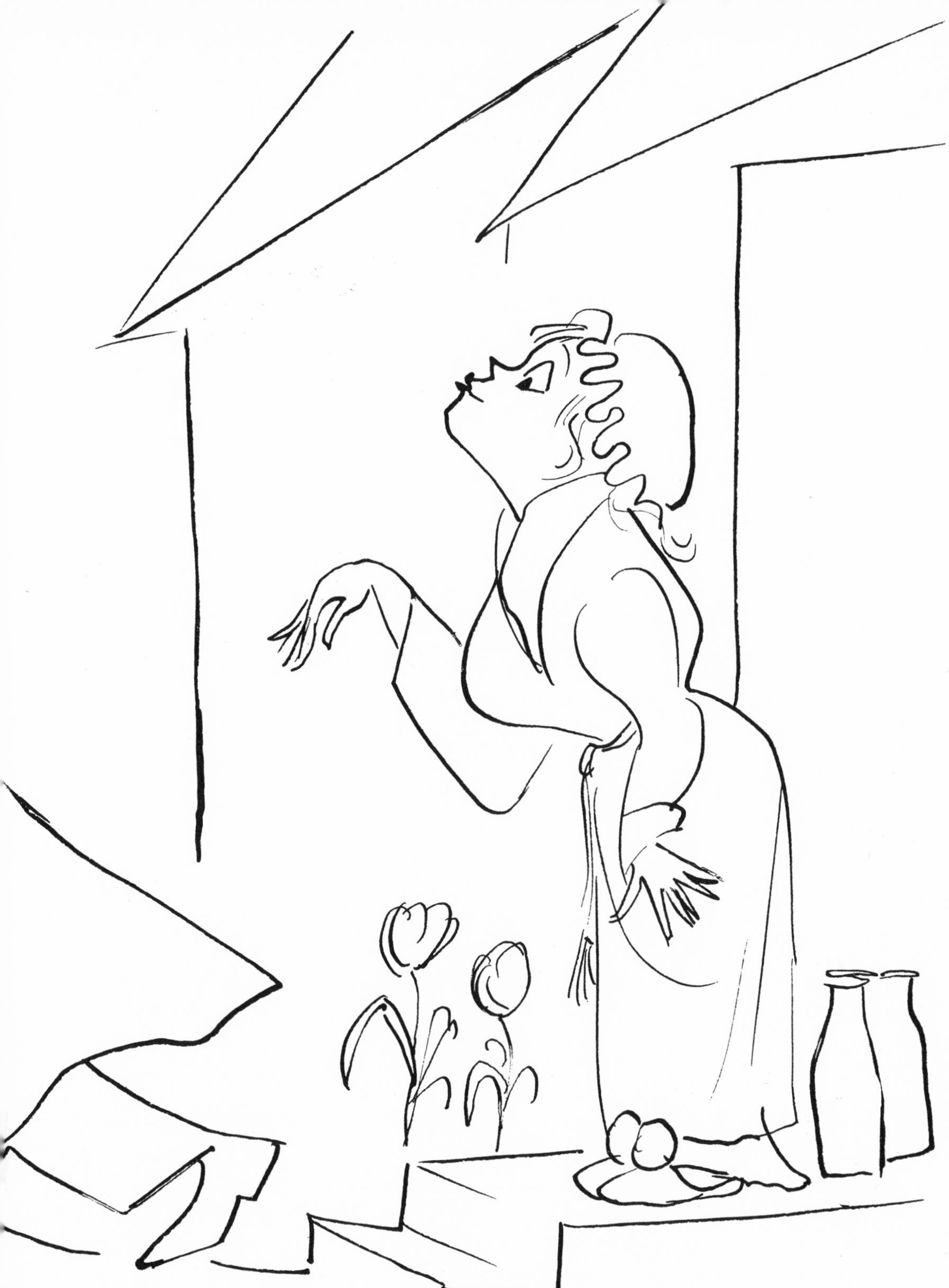

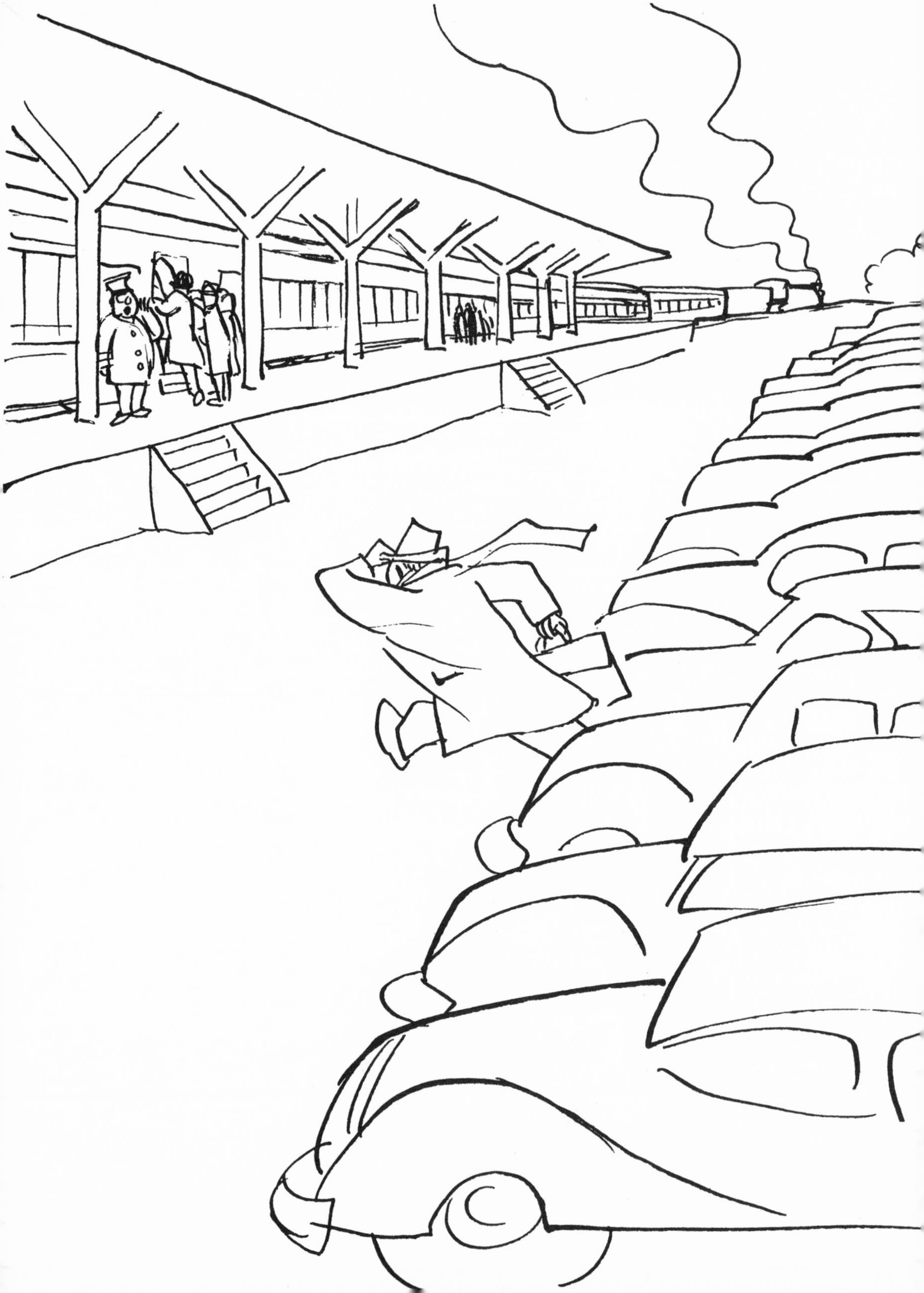

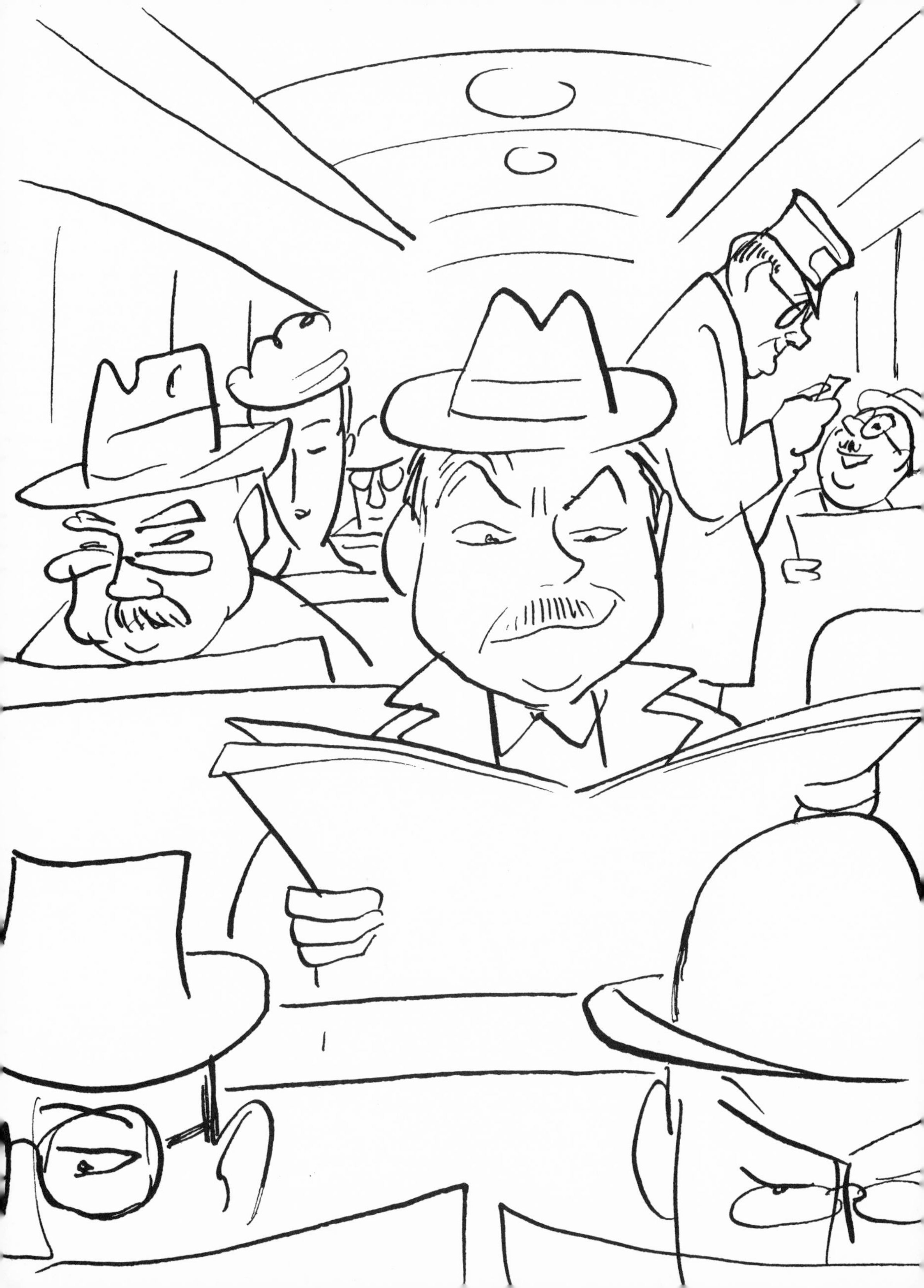

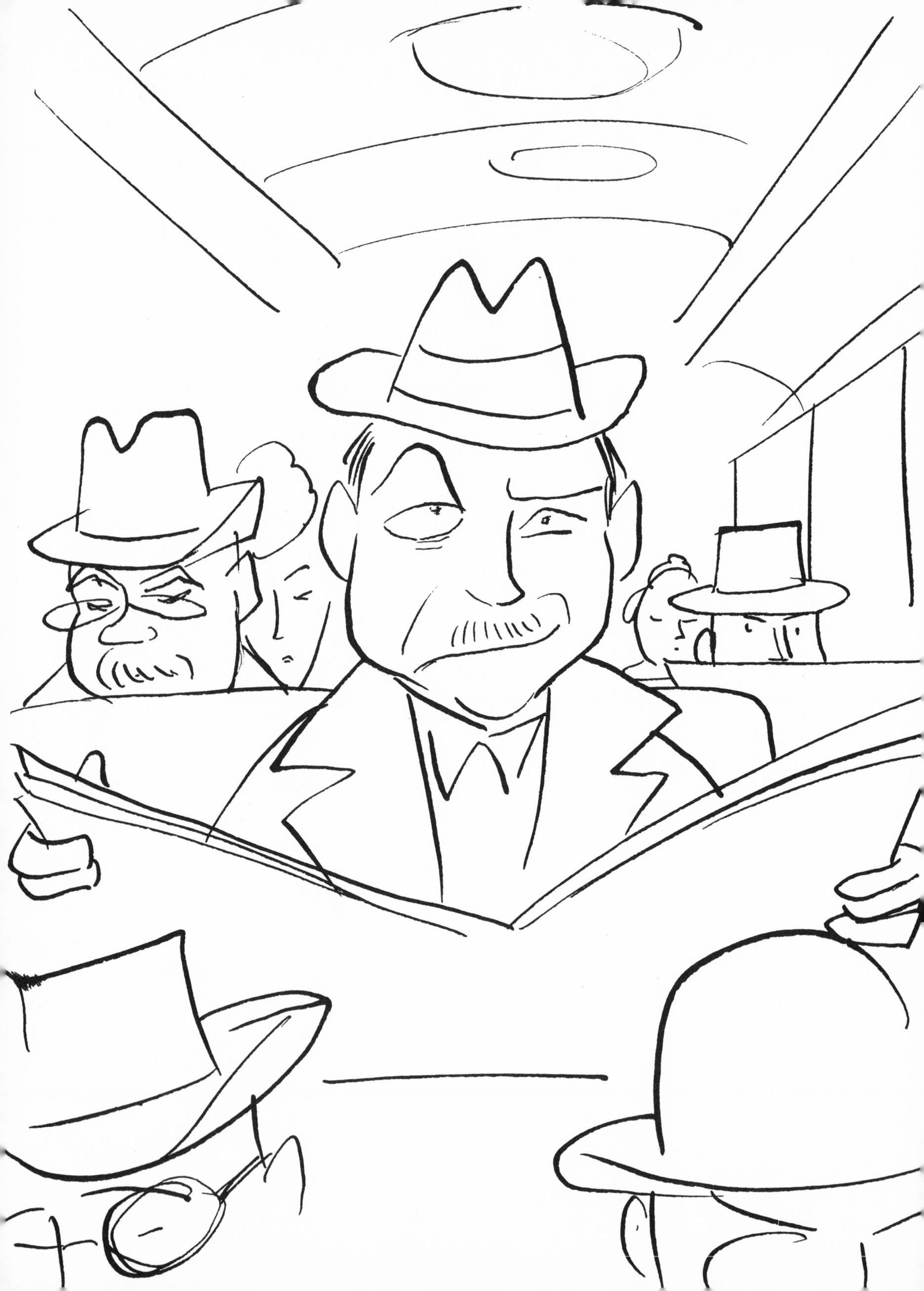

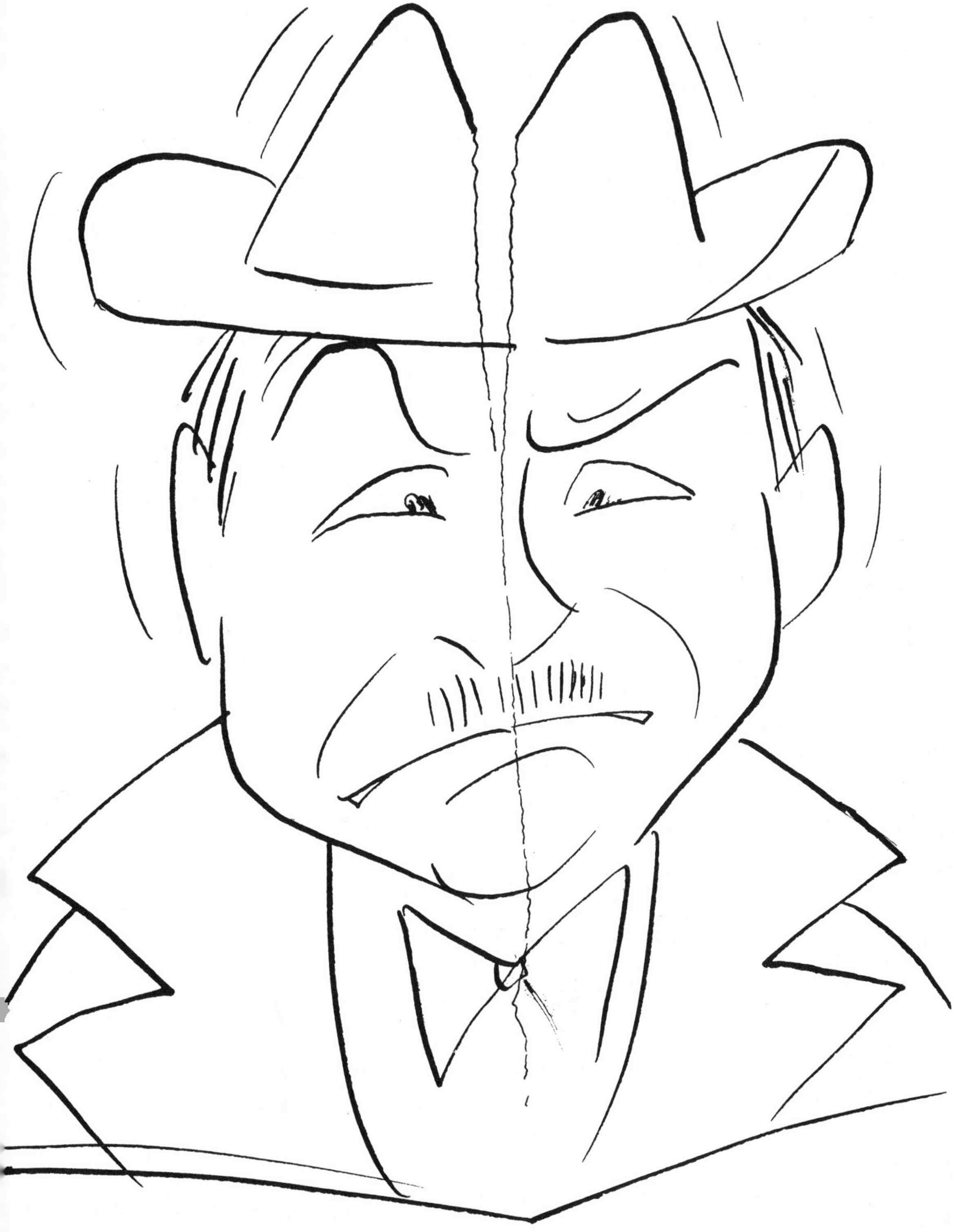

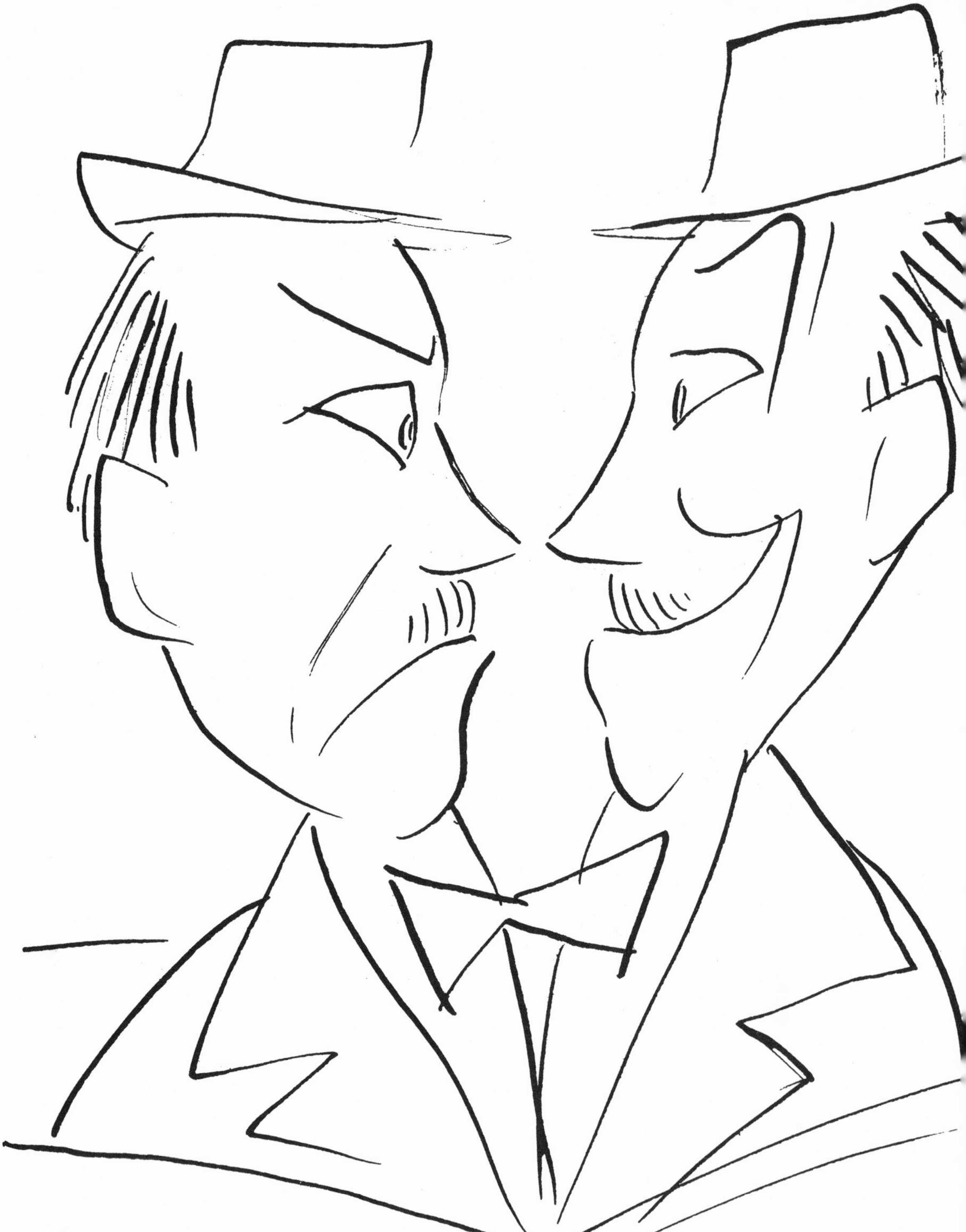

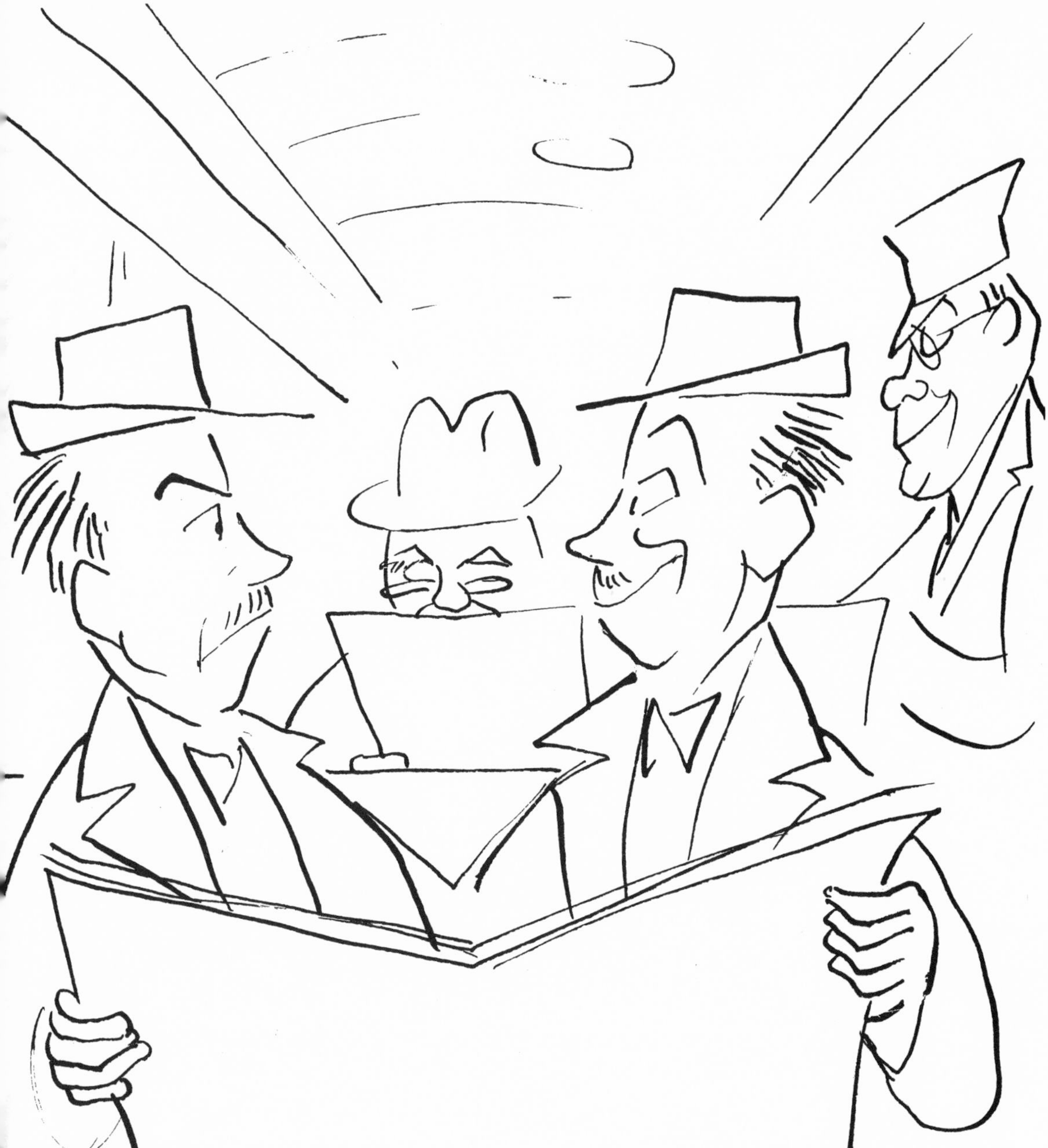

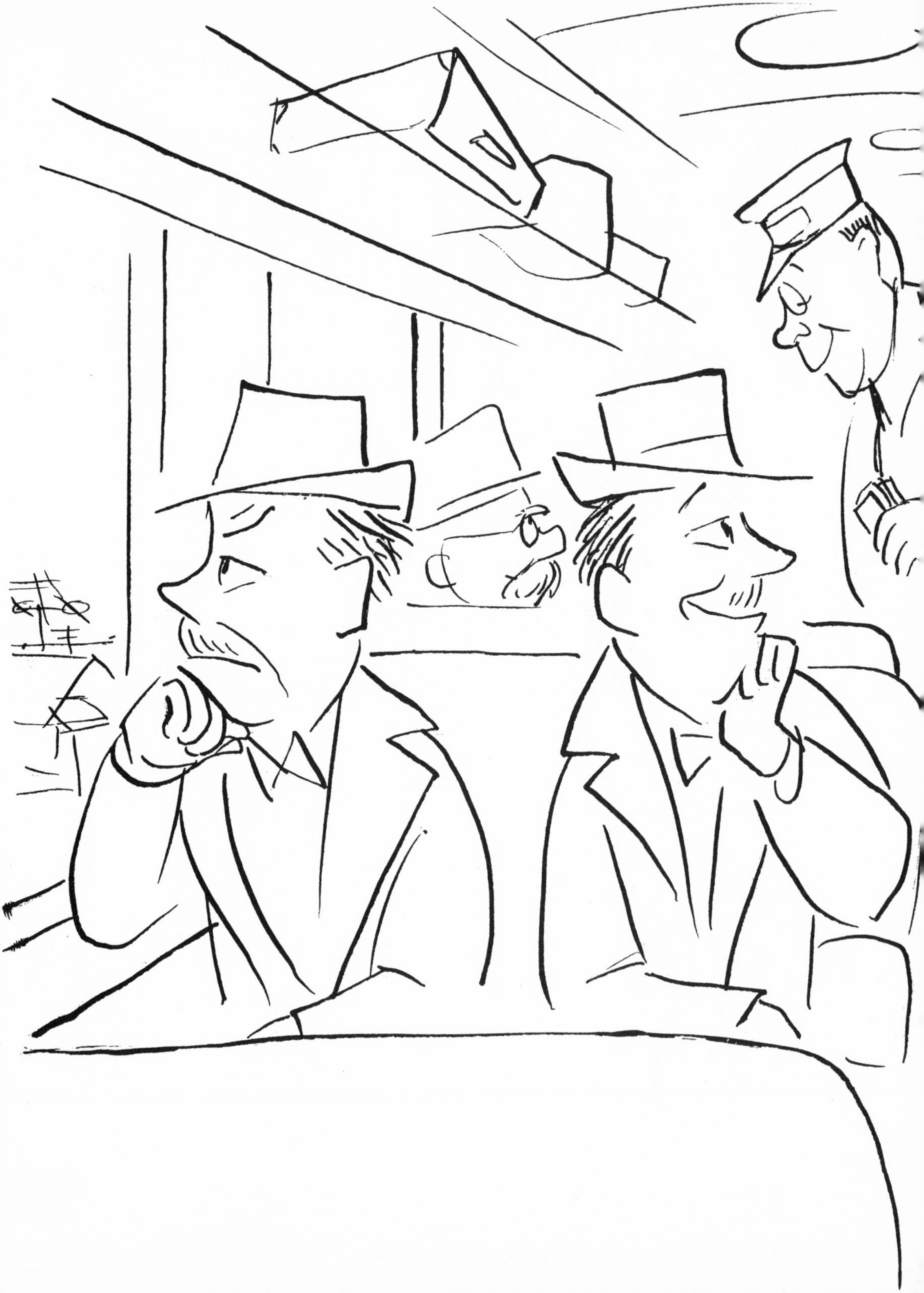

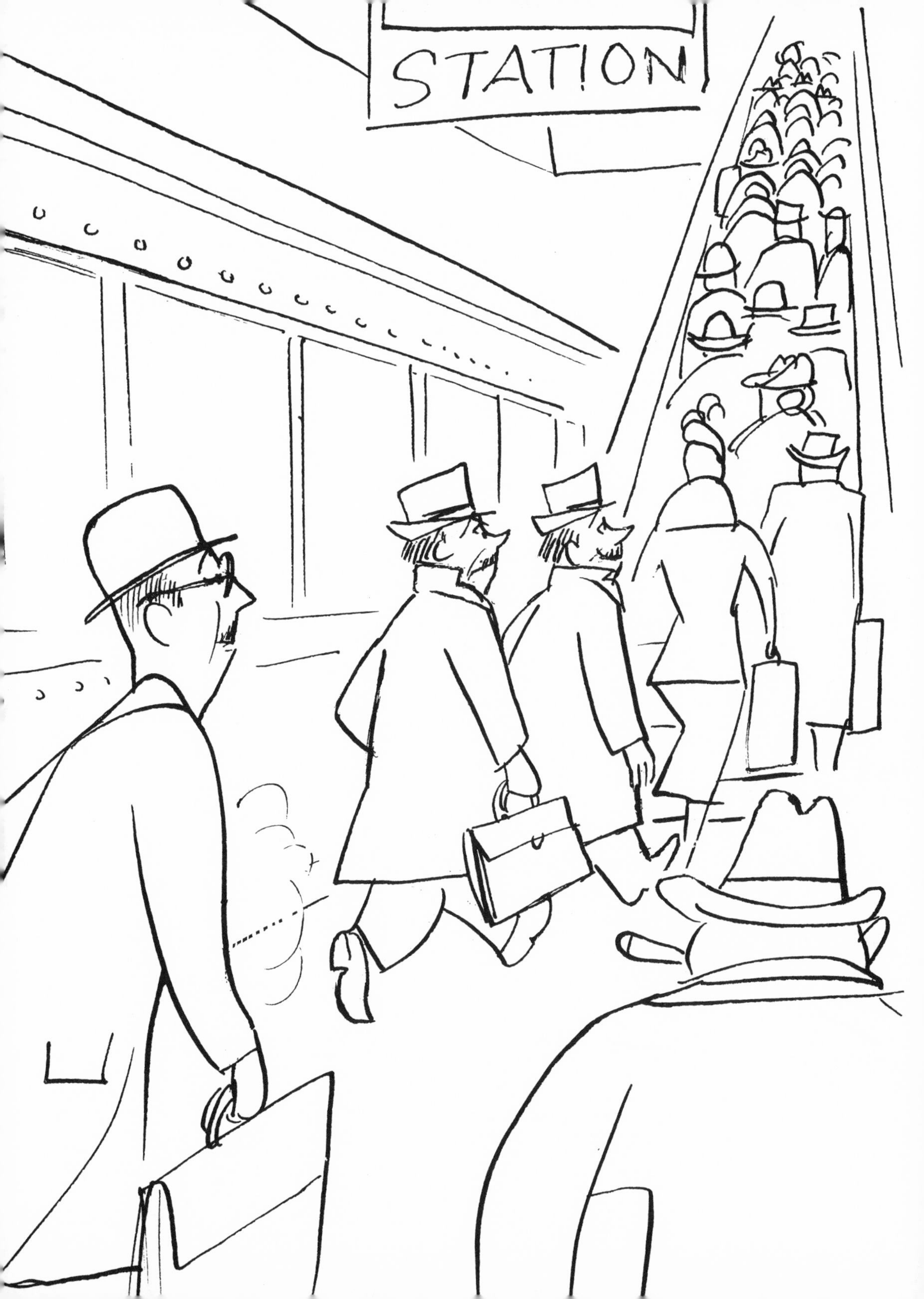
STATION

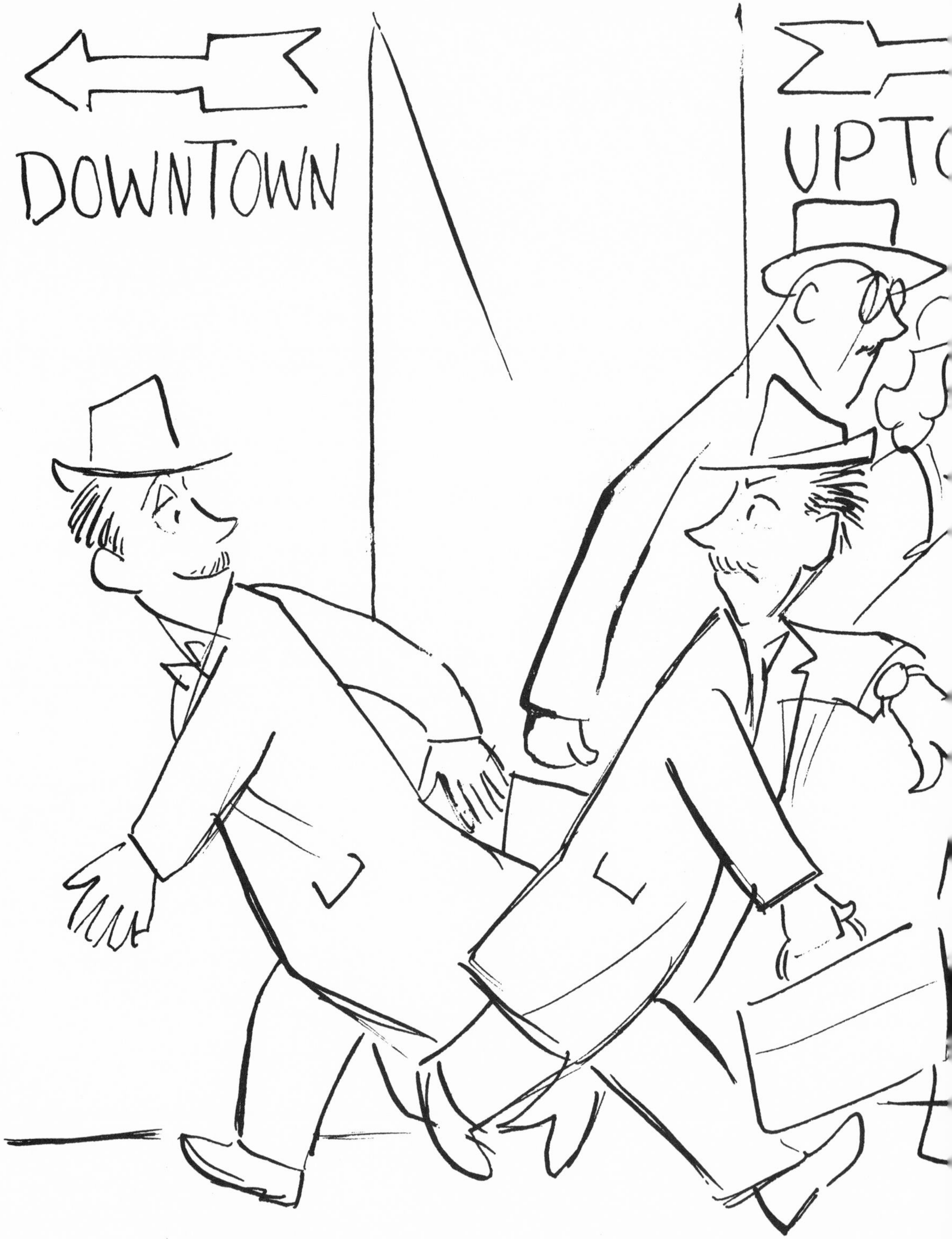

DOWNTOWN
UPTO

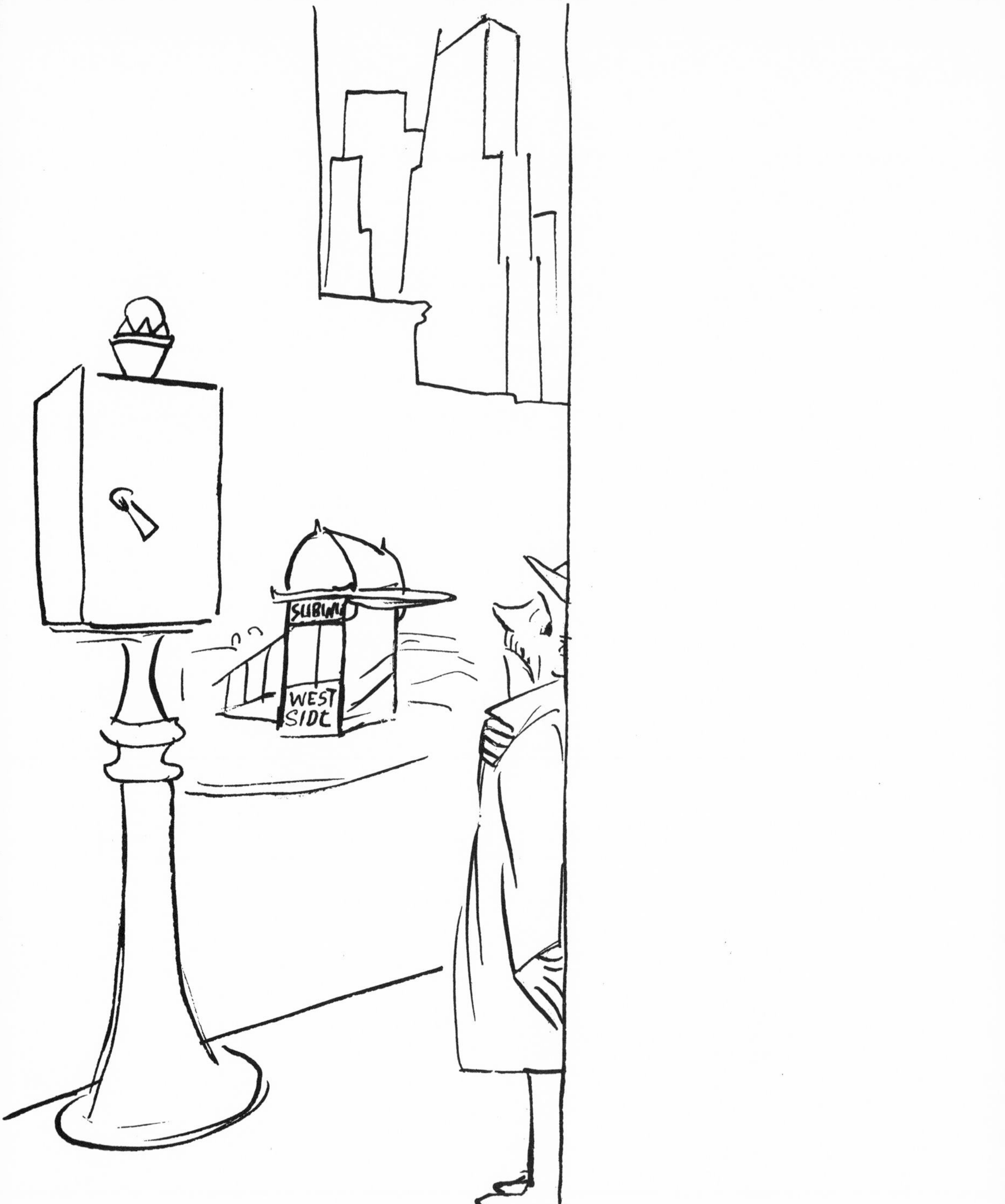
SUBWAY
WEST
SIDE

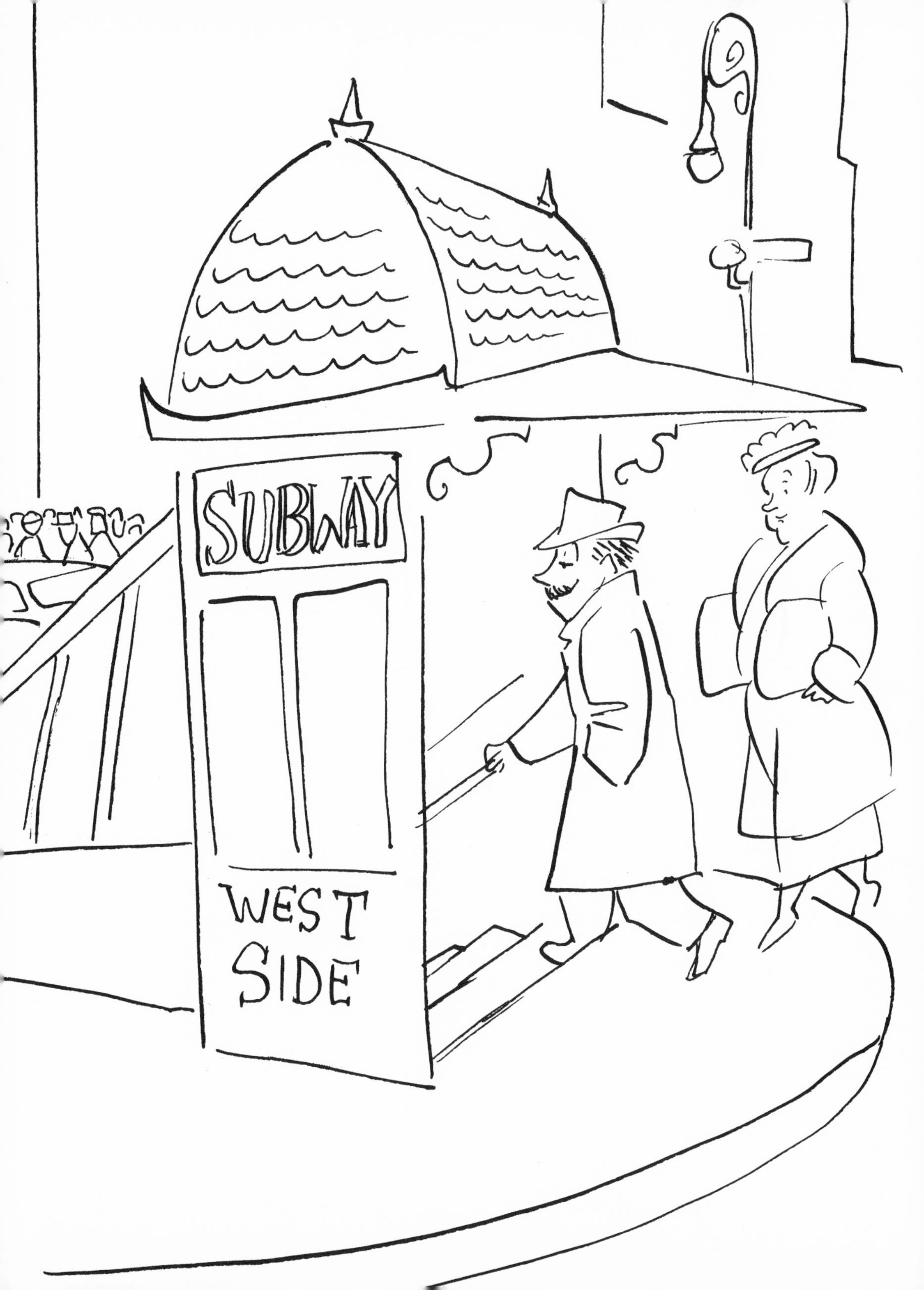
SUBWAY
WEST
SIDE

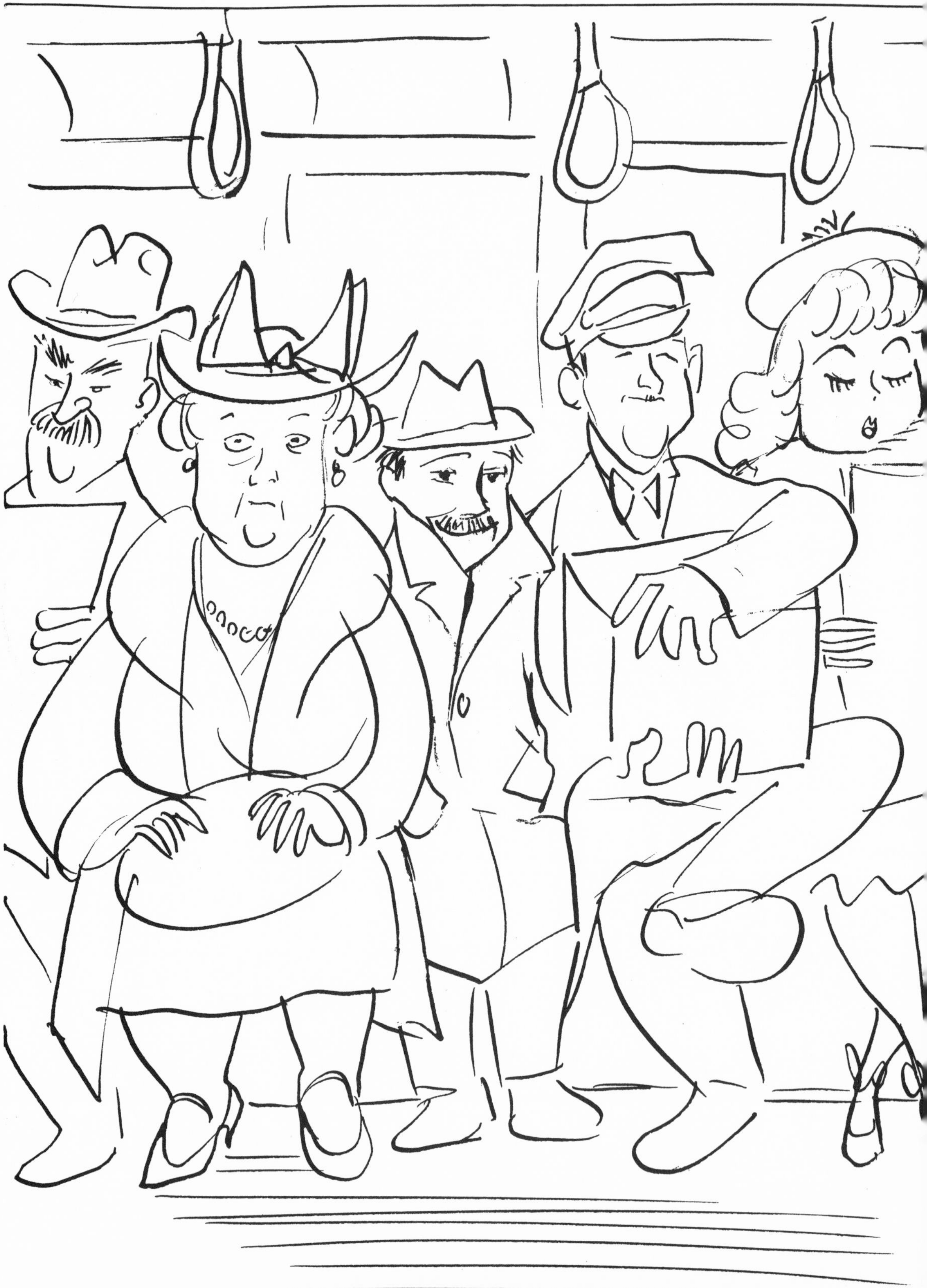

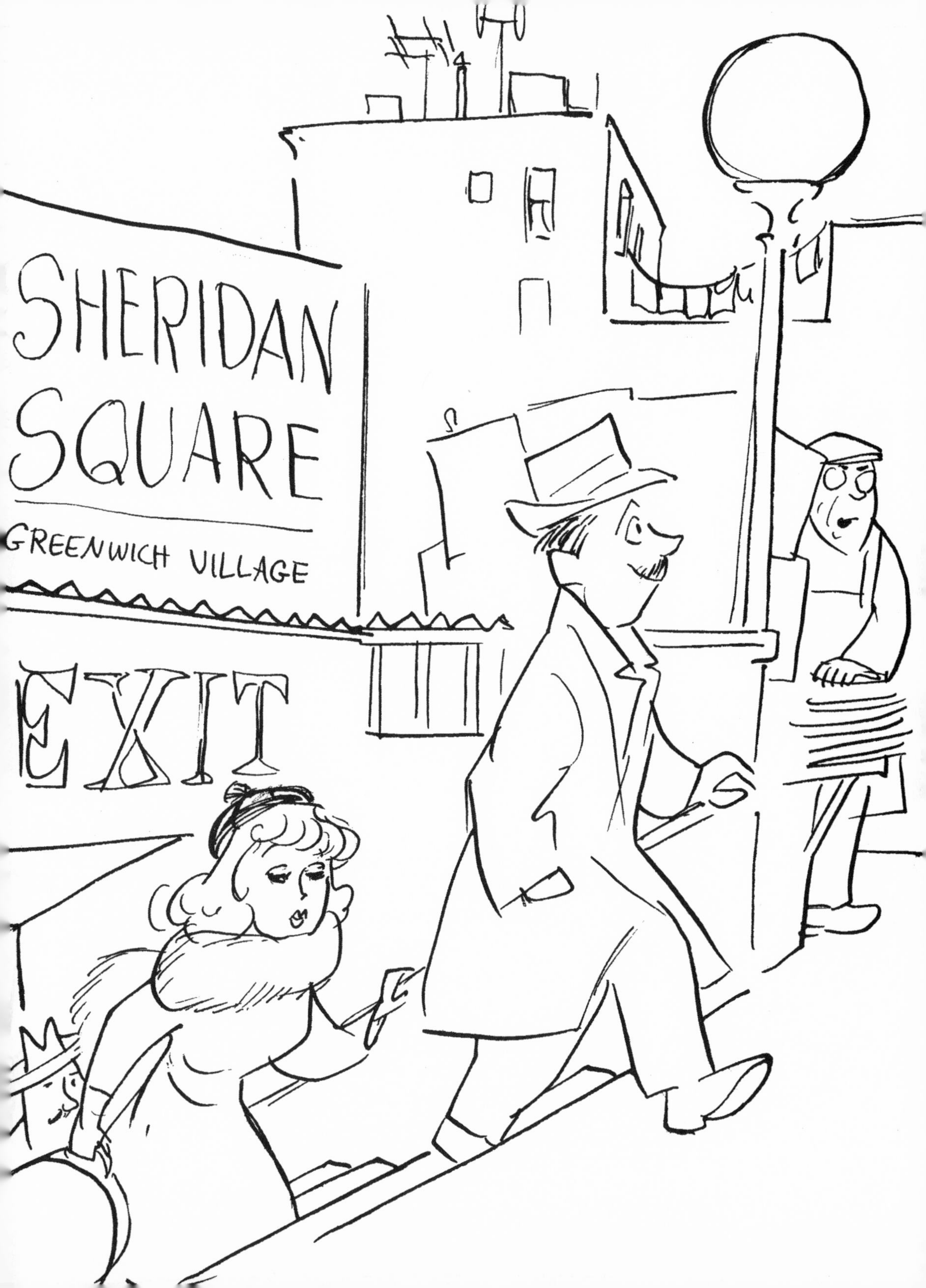
SHERIDAN
SQUARE
GREENWICH VILLAGE
EXIT

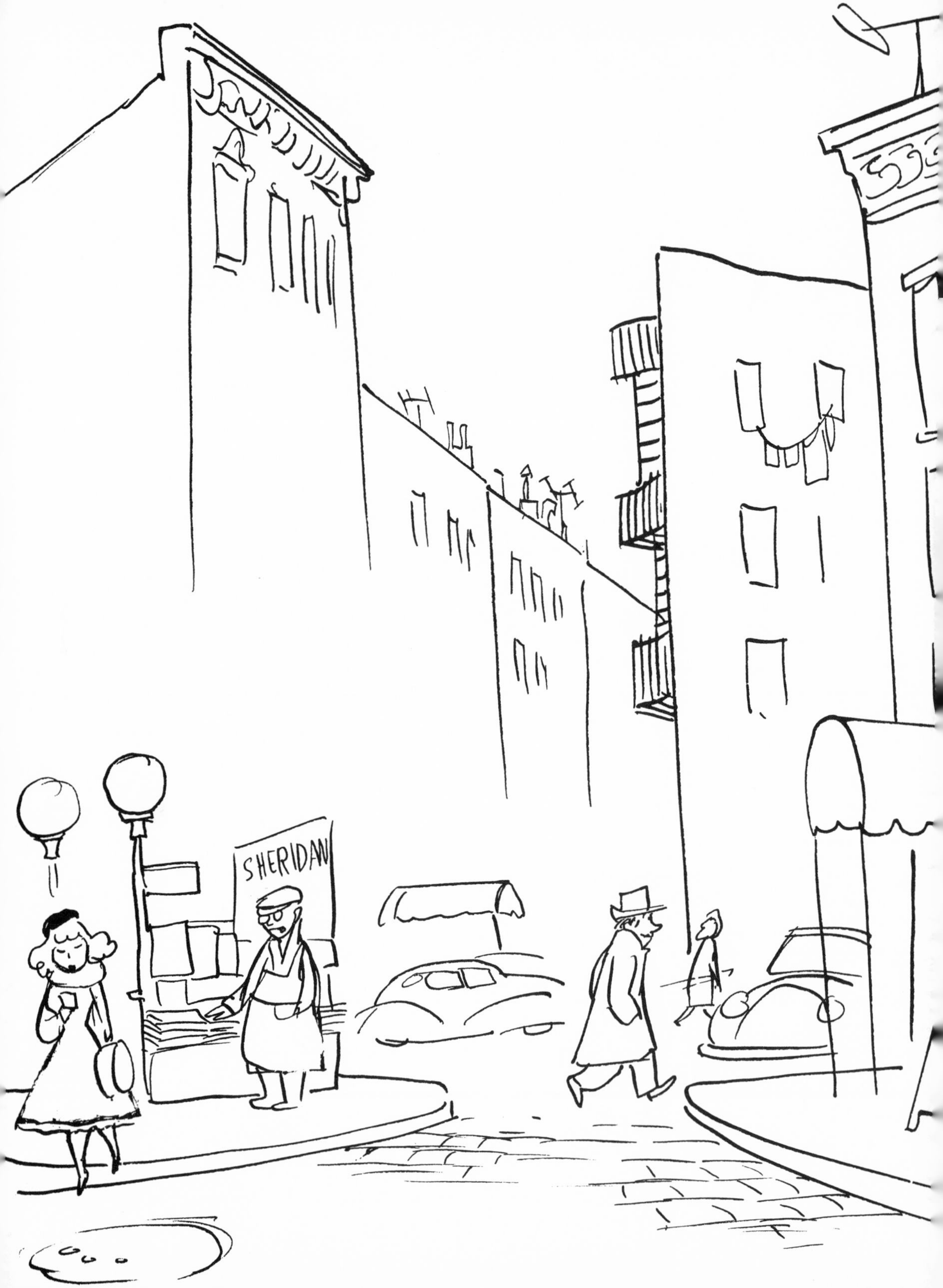
SHERIDAN

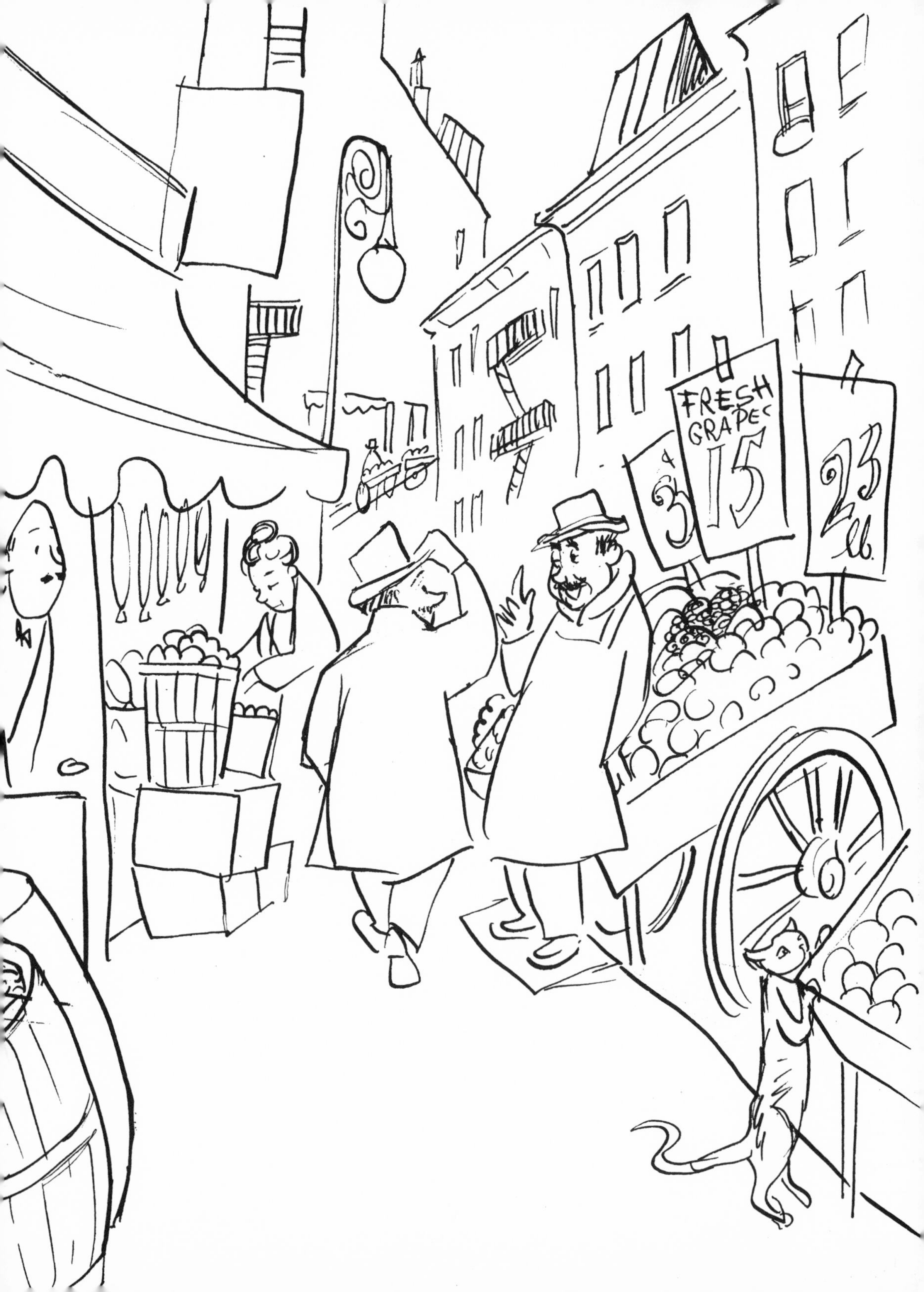
FRESH
GRAPES
15
3
23
lb.

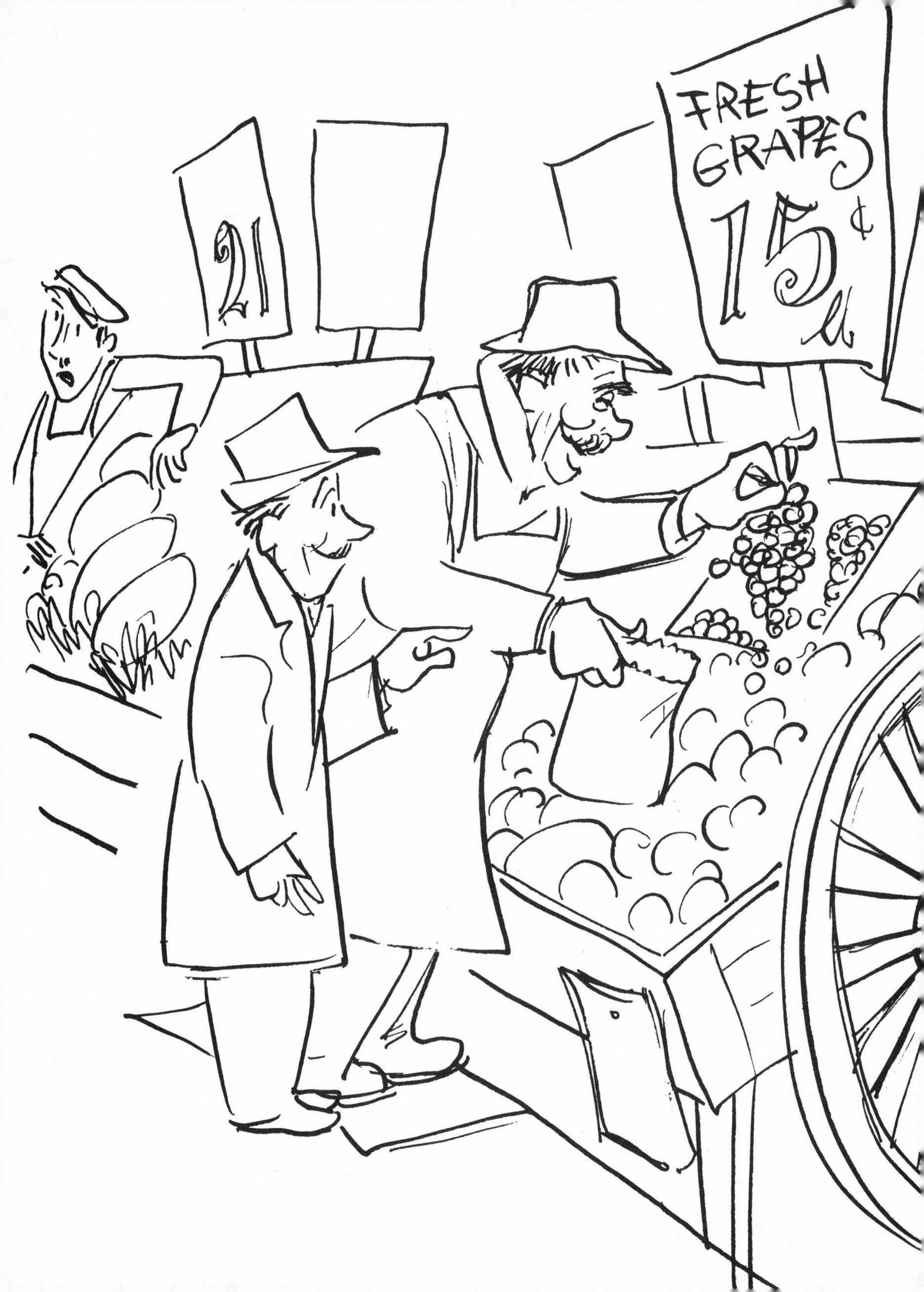
21
FRESH GRAPES 15¢

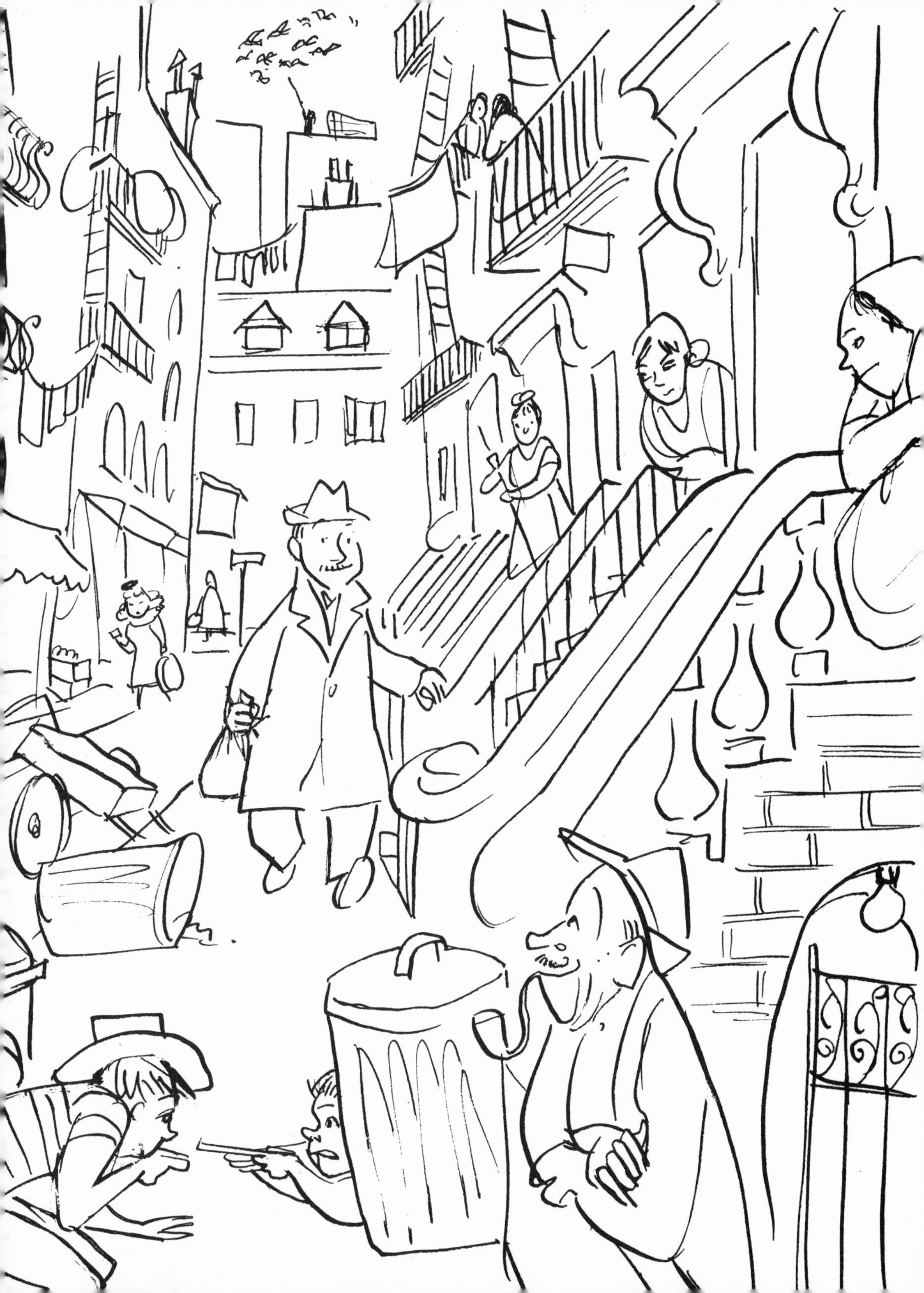

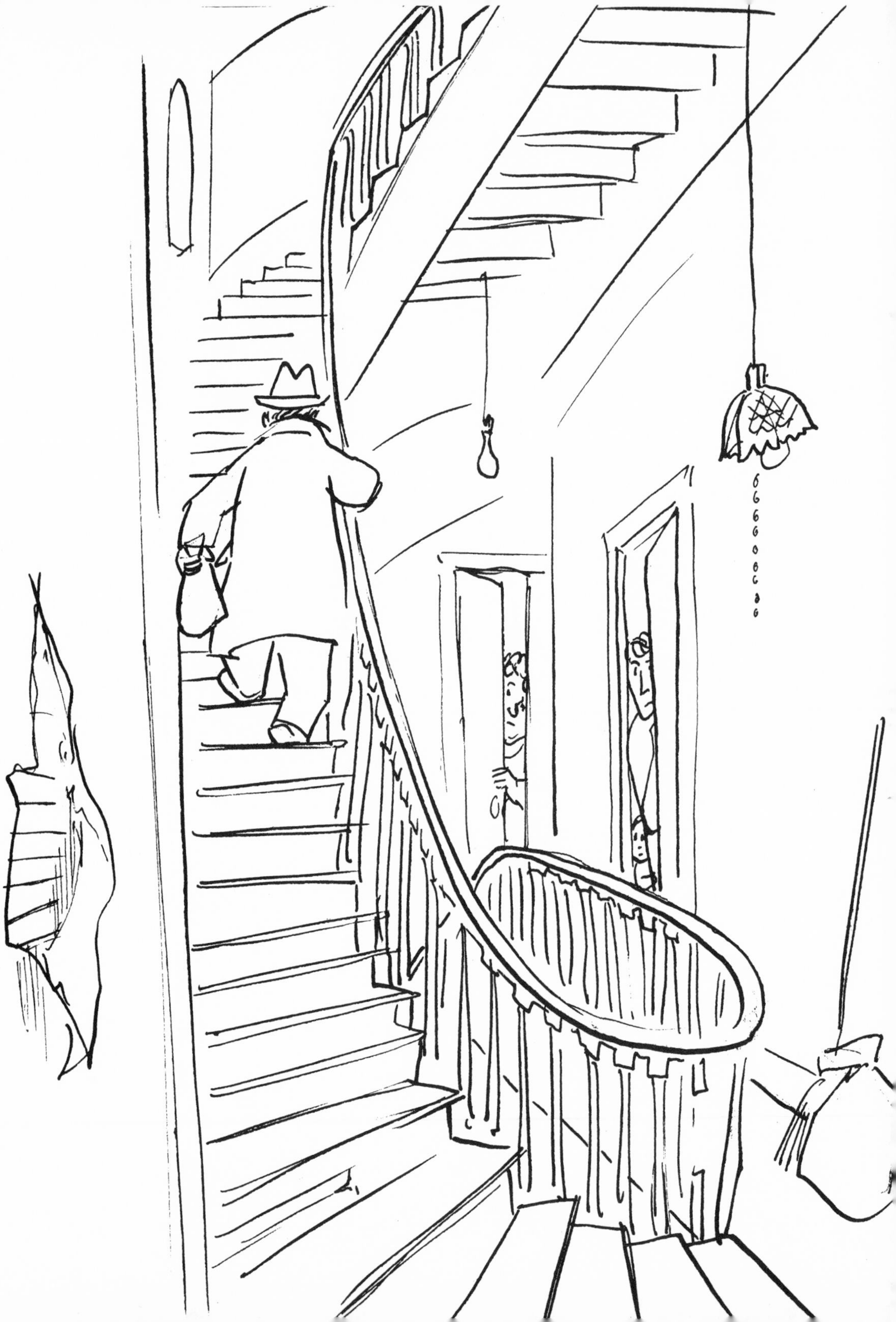

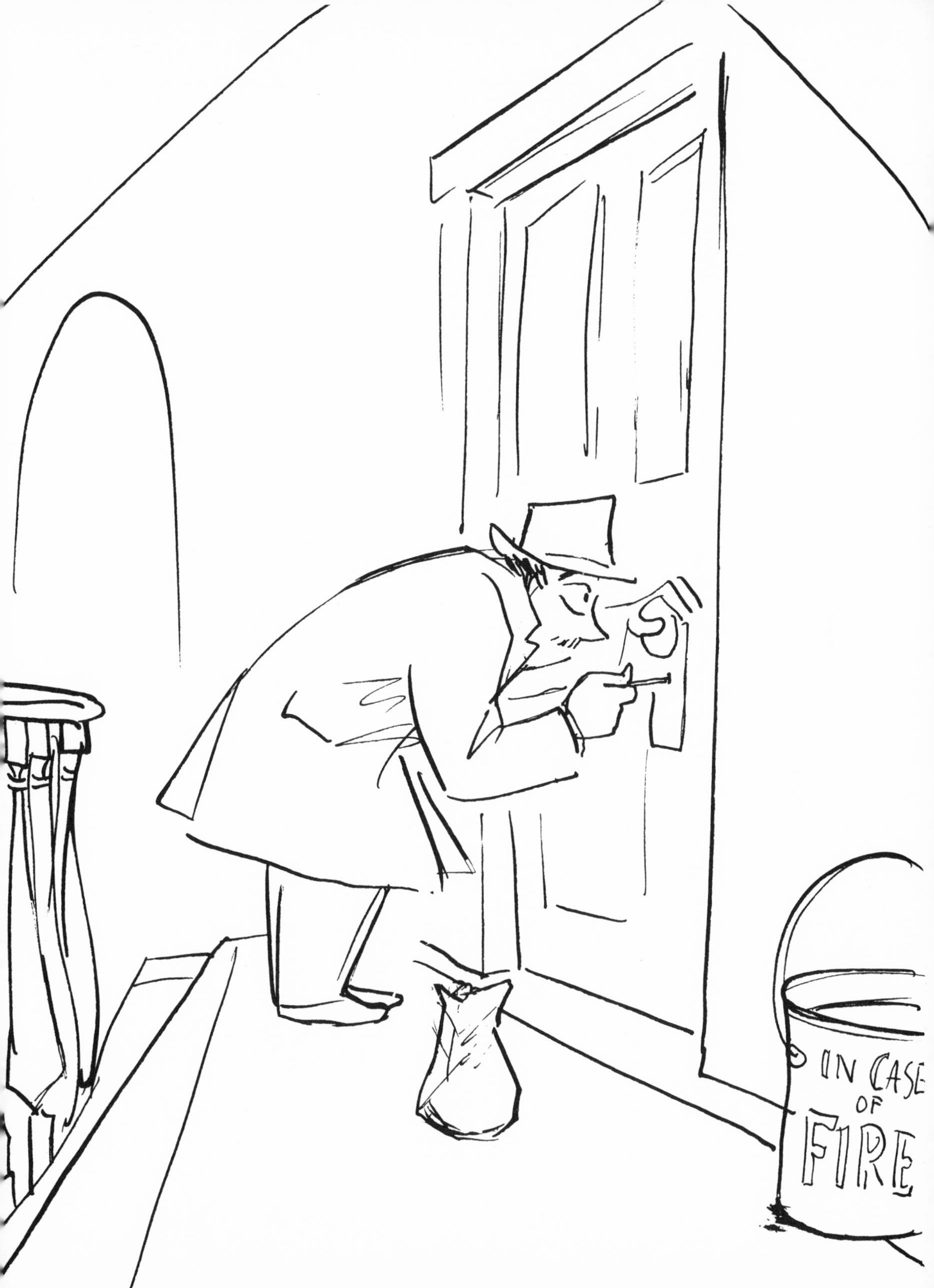
IN CASE
OF
FIRE

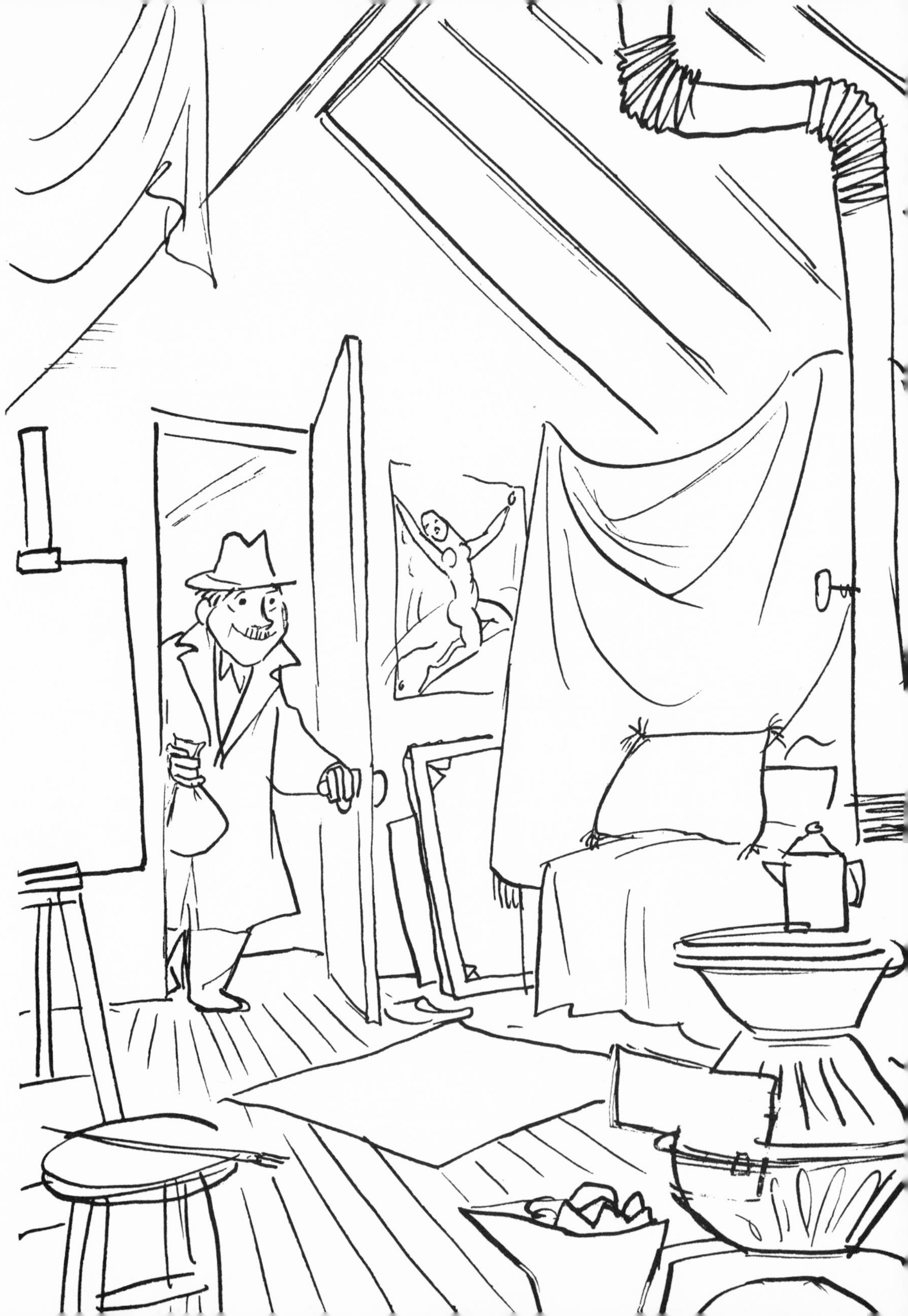

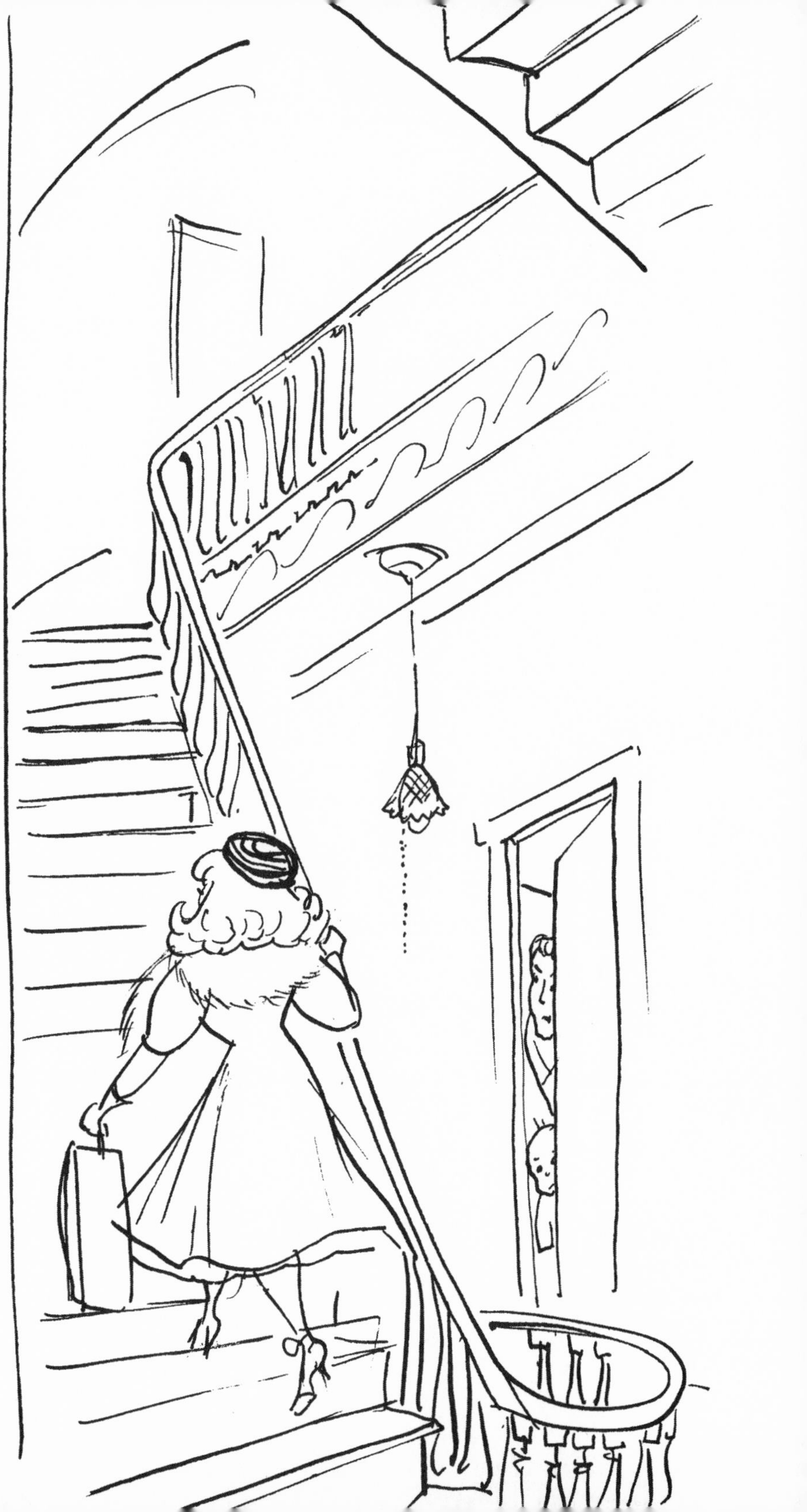

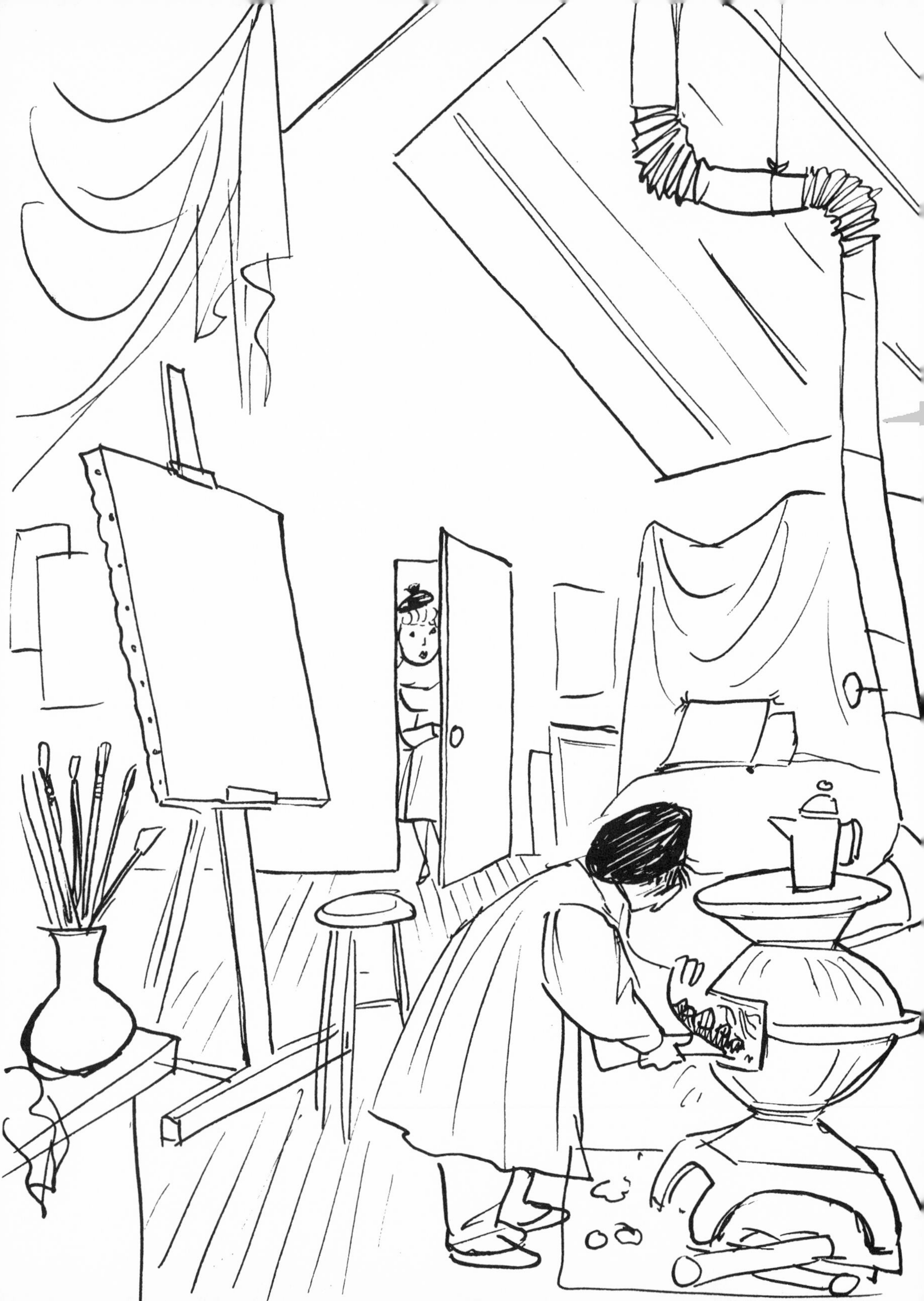

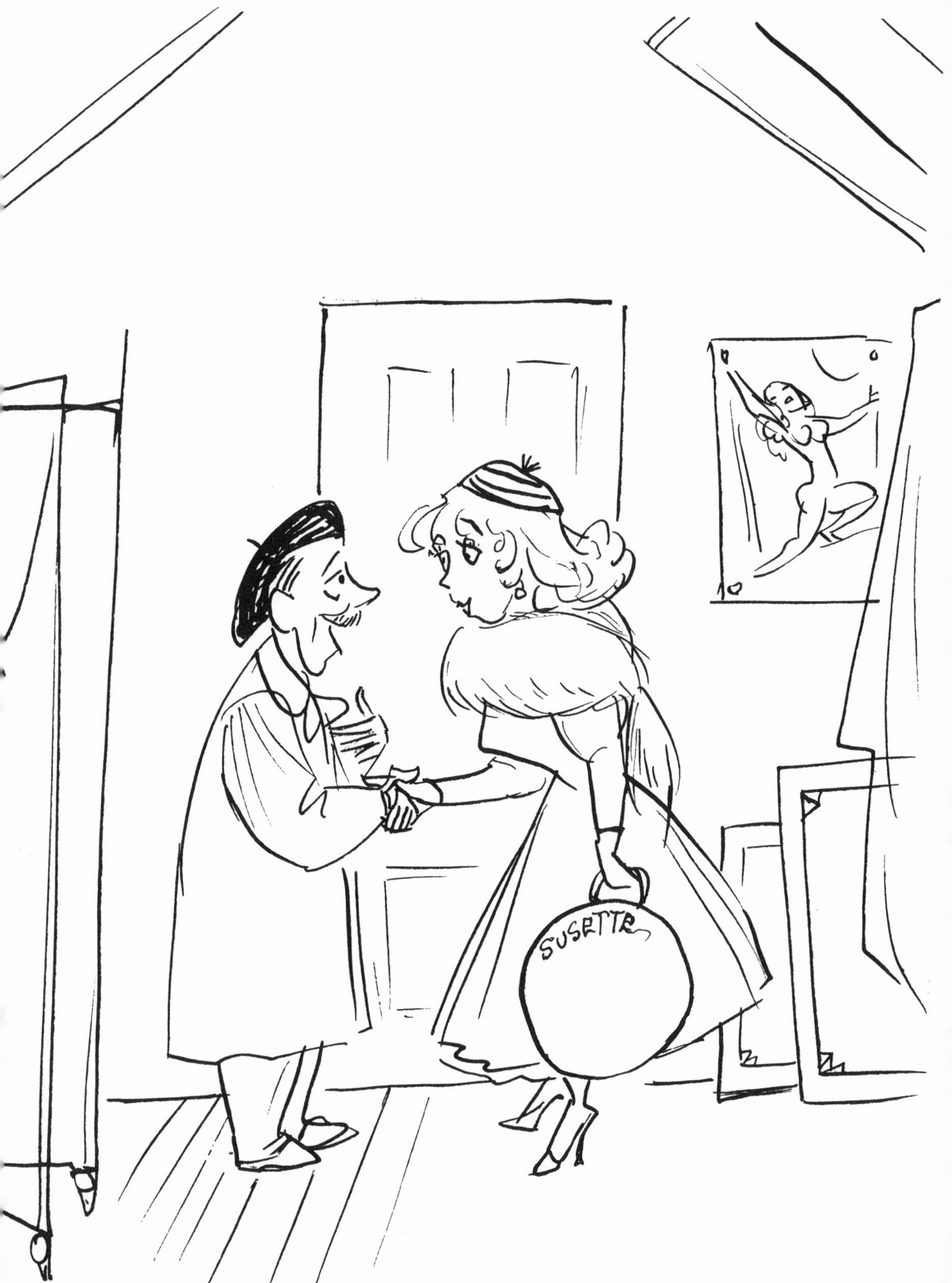
SUSETTE

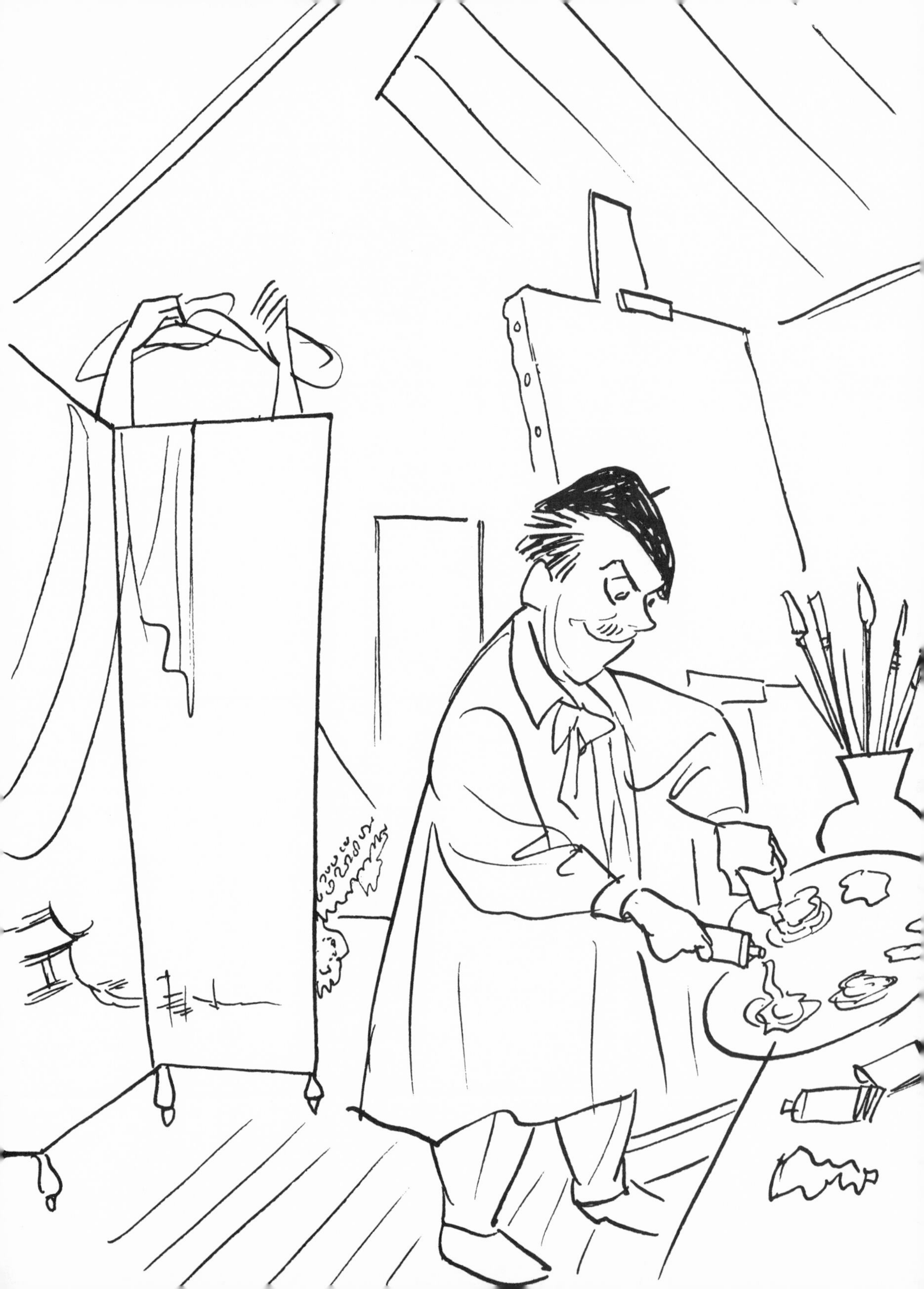

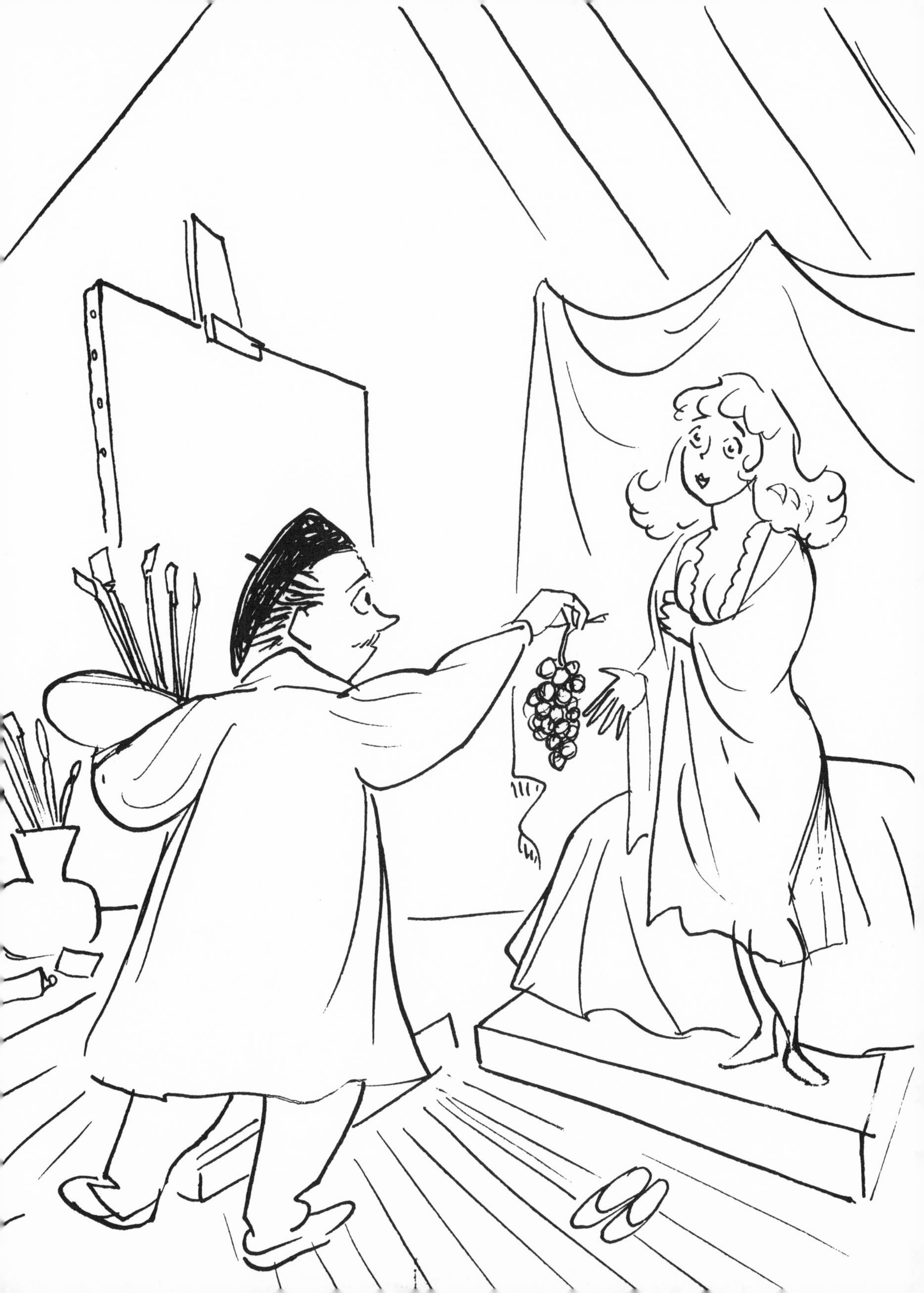

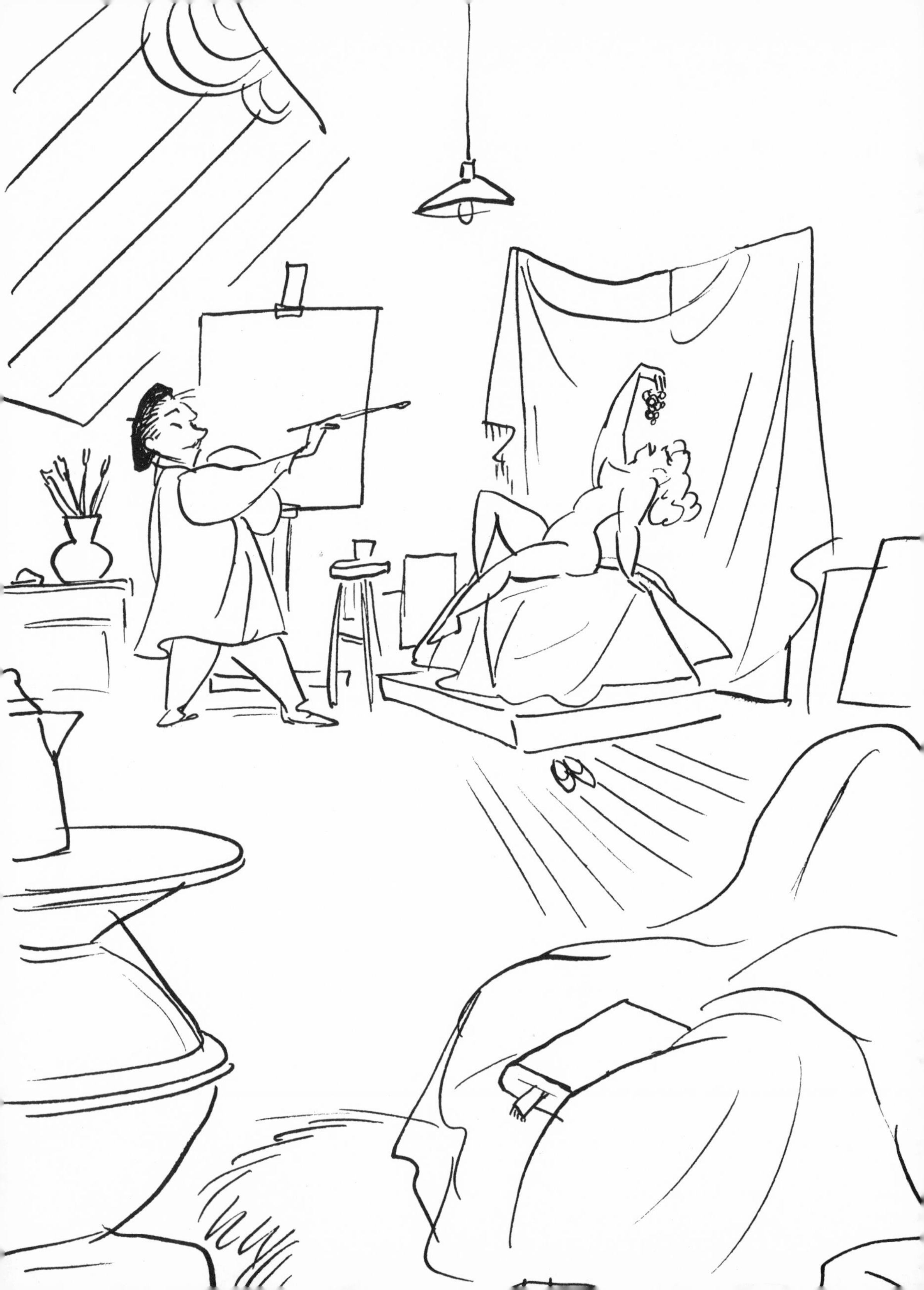

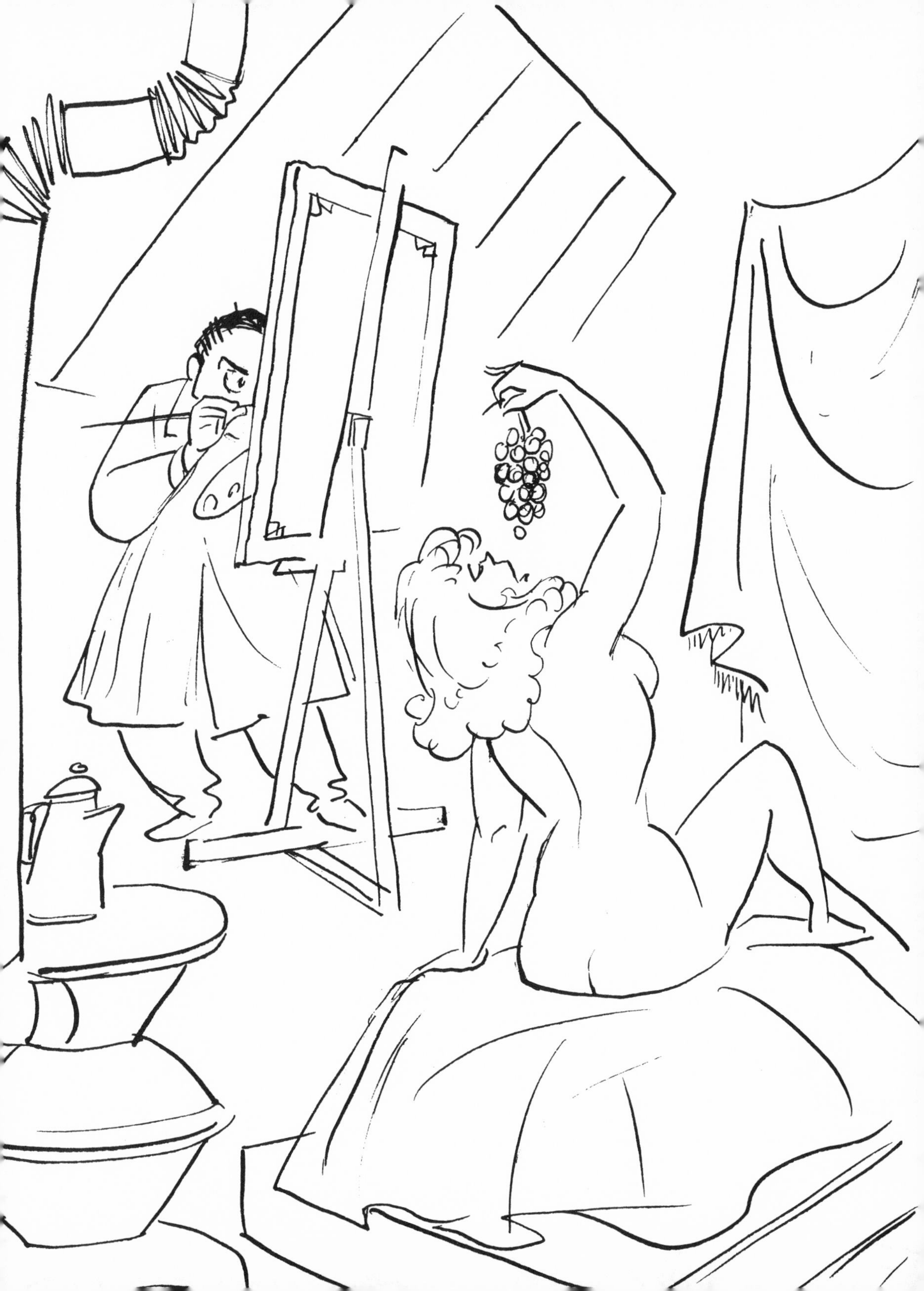

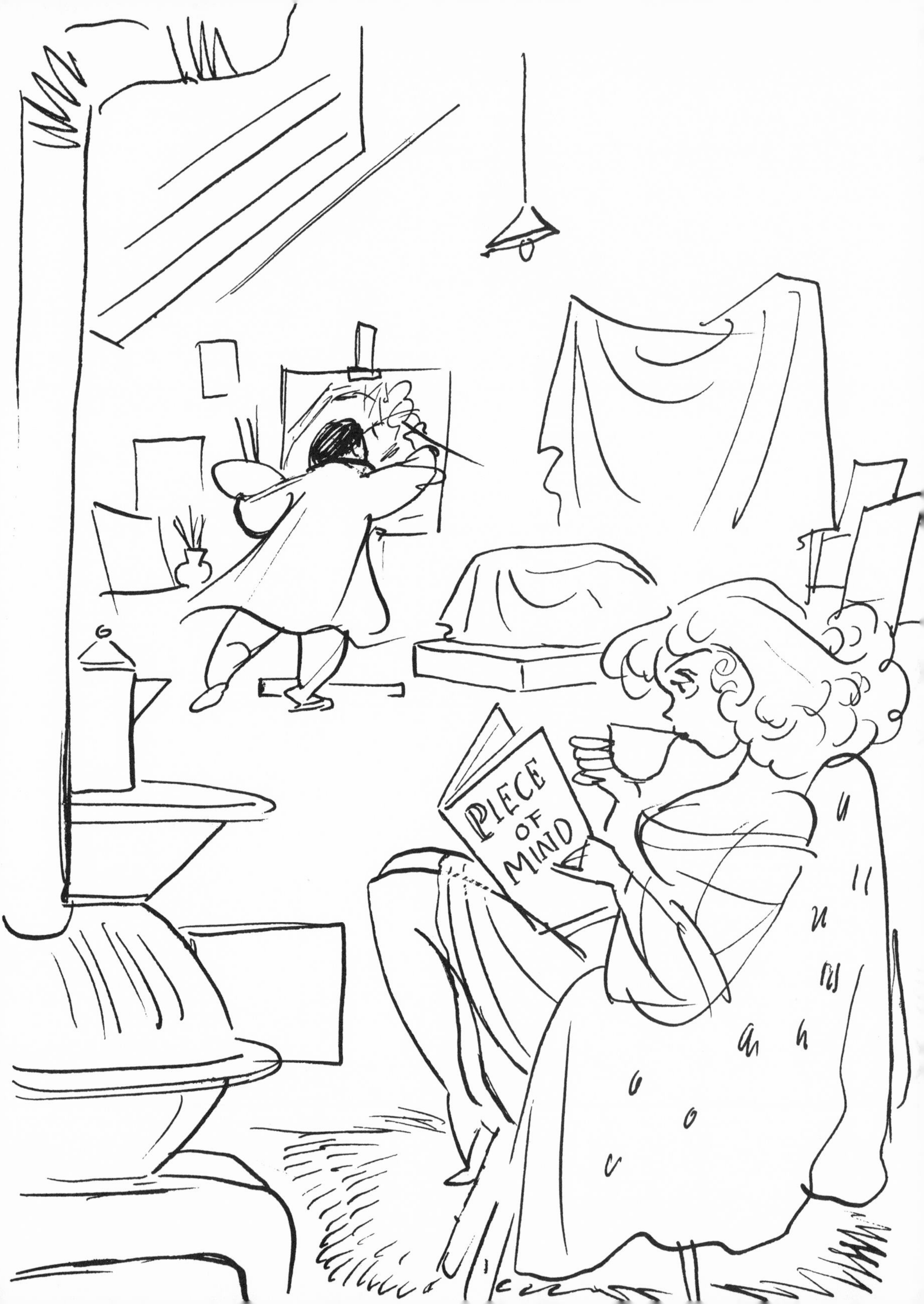
PIECE OF MIND

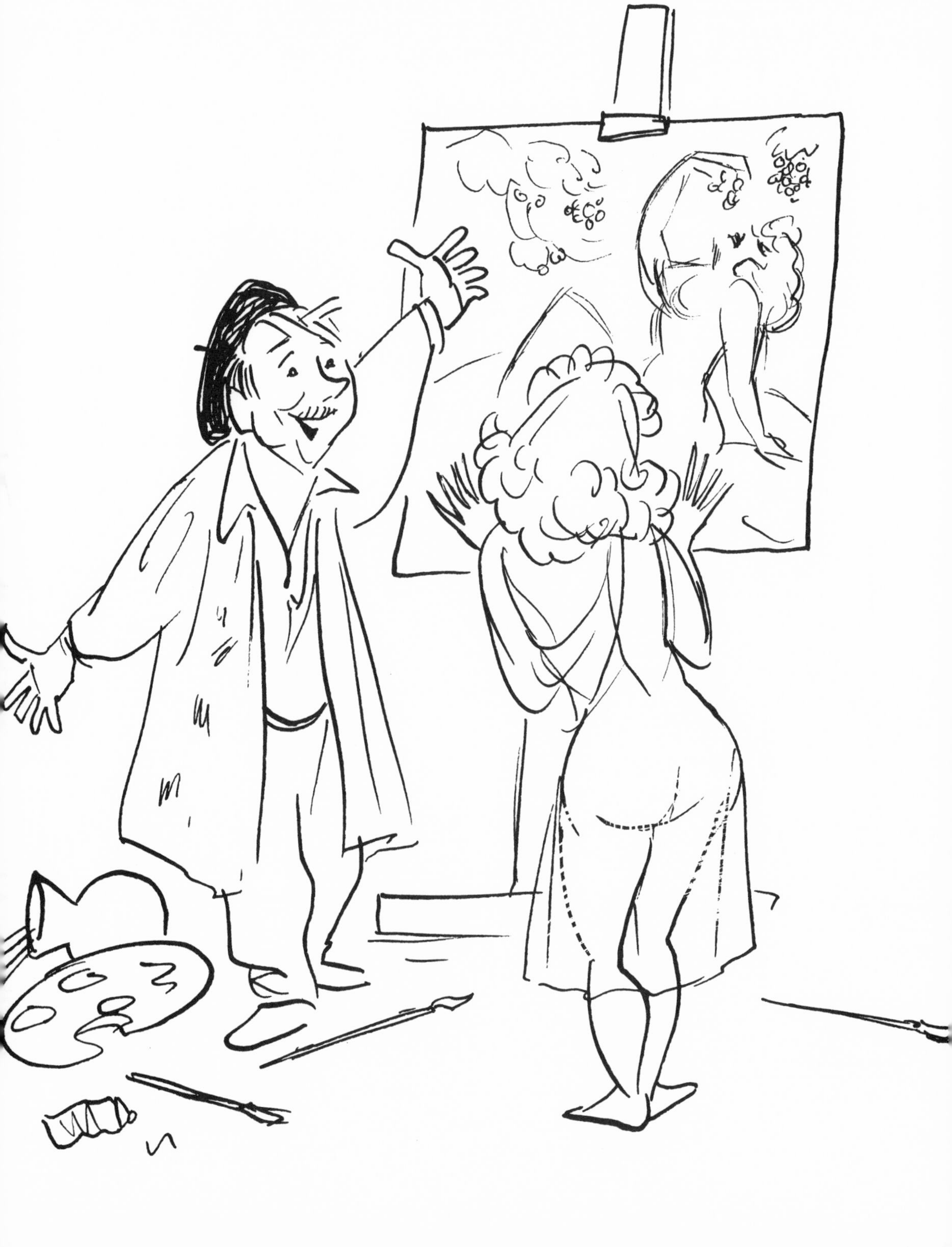

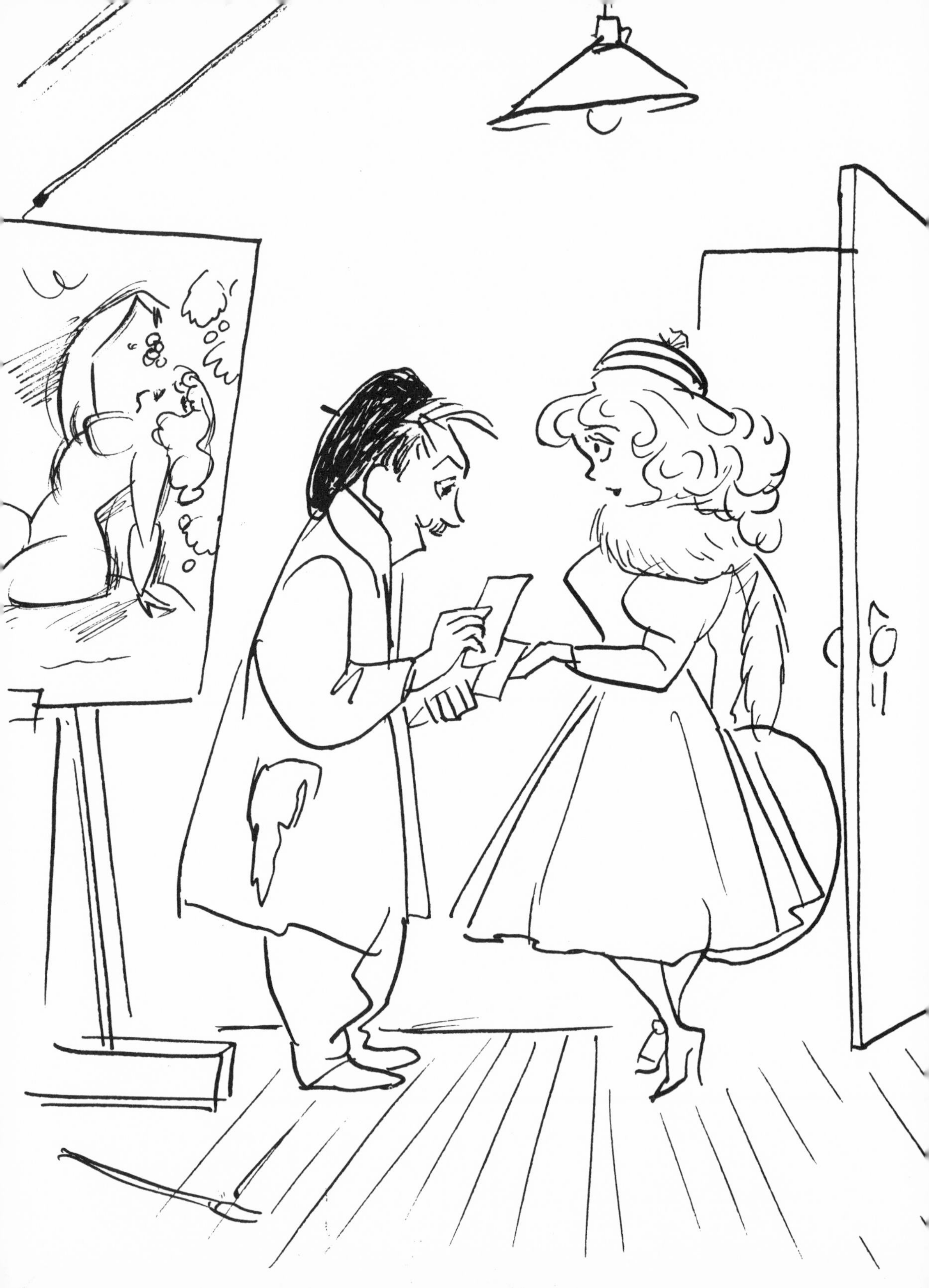

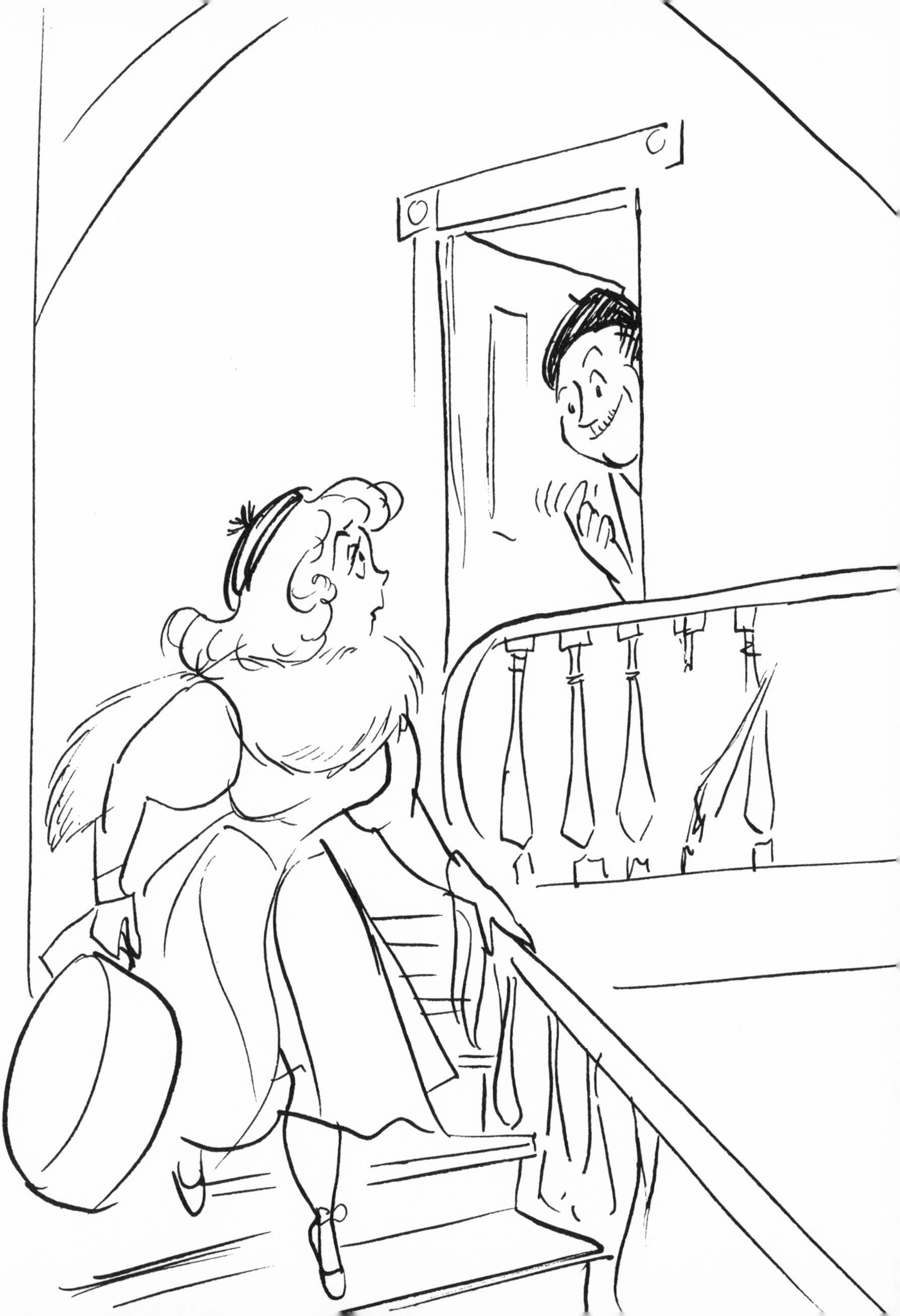

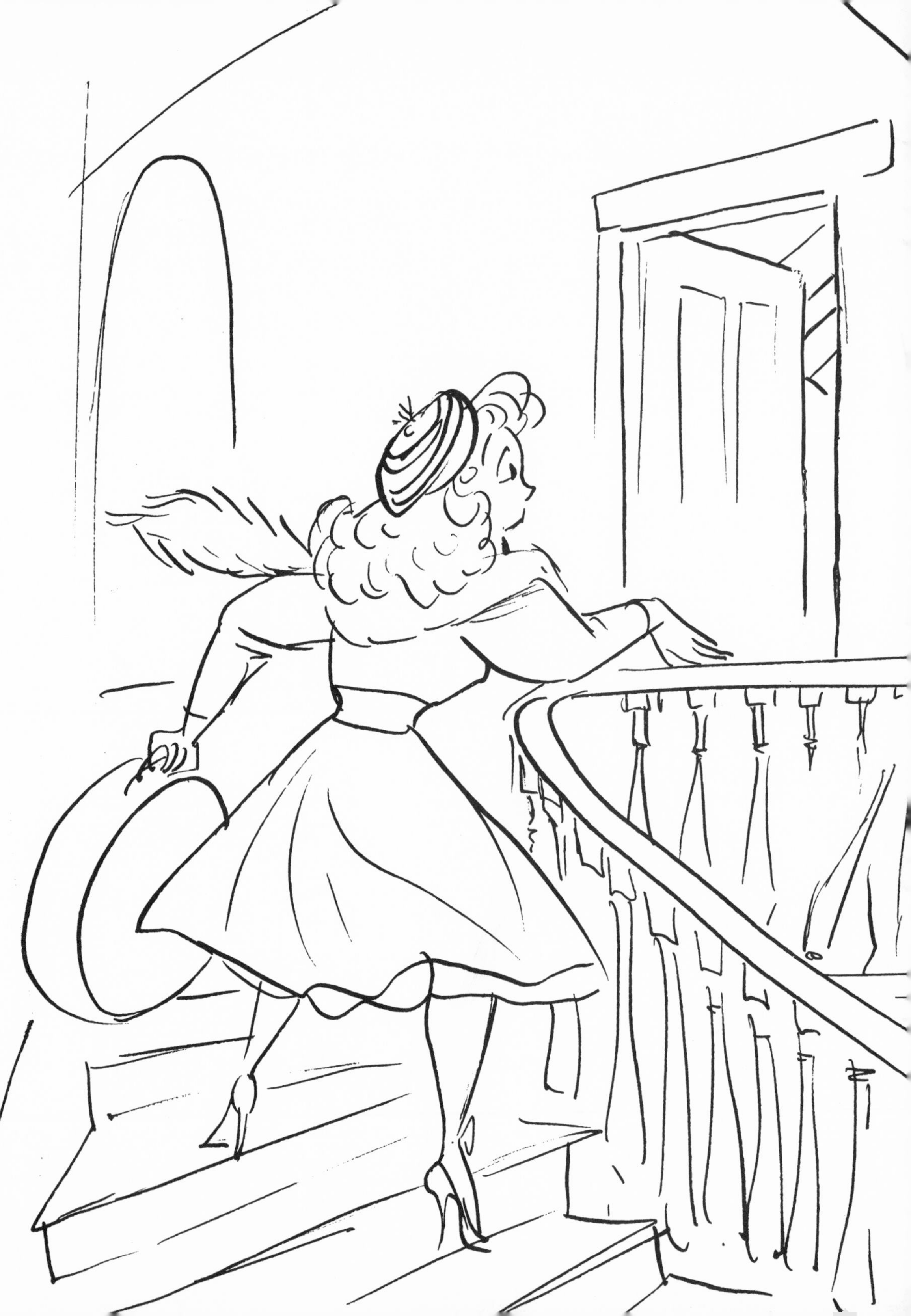

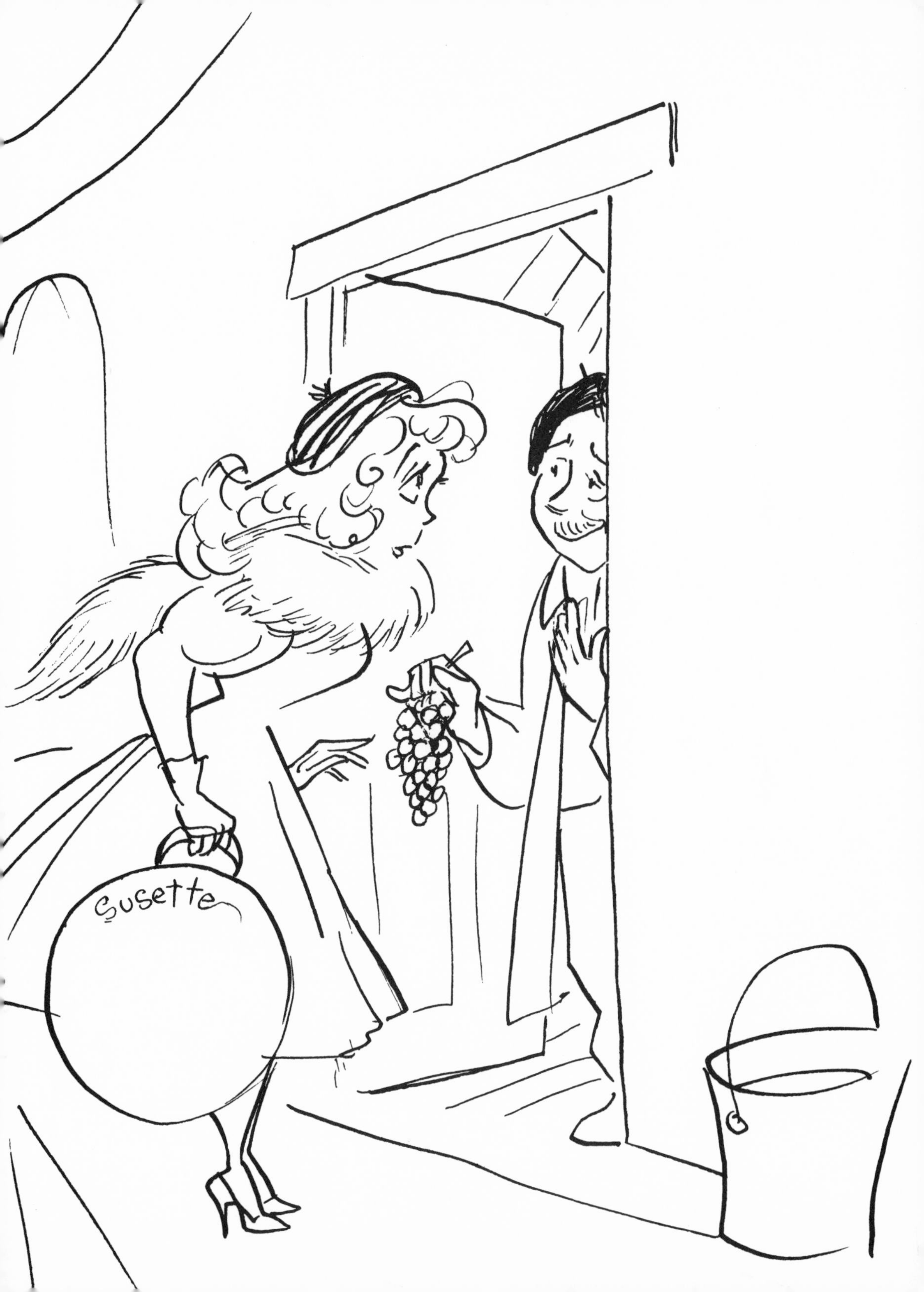
Susette

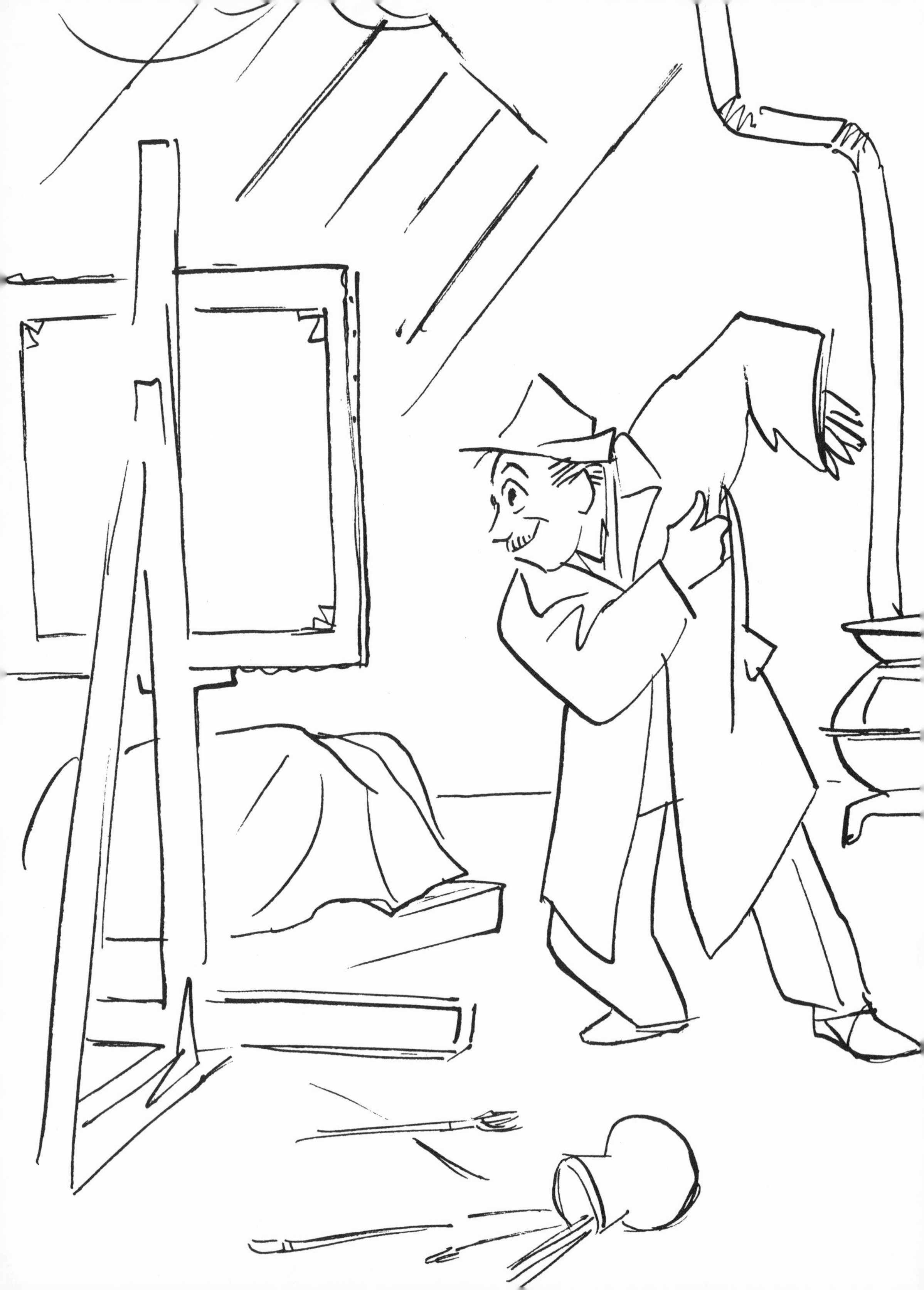

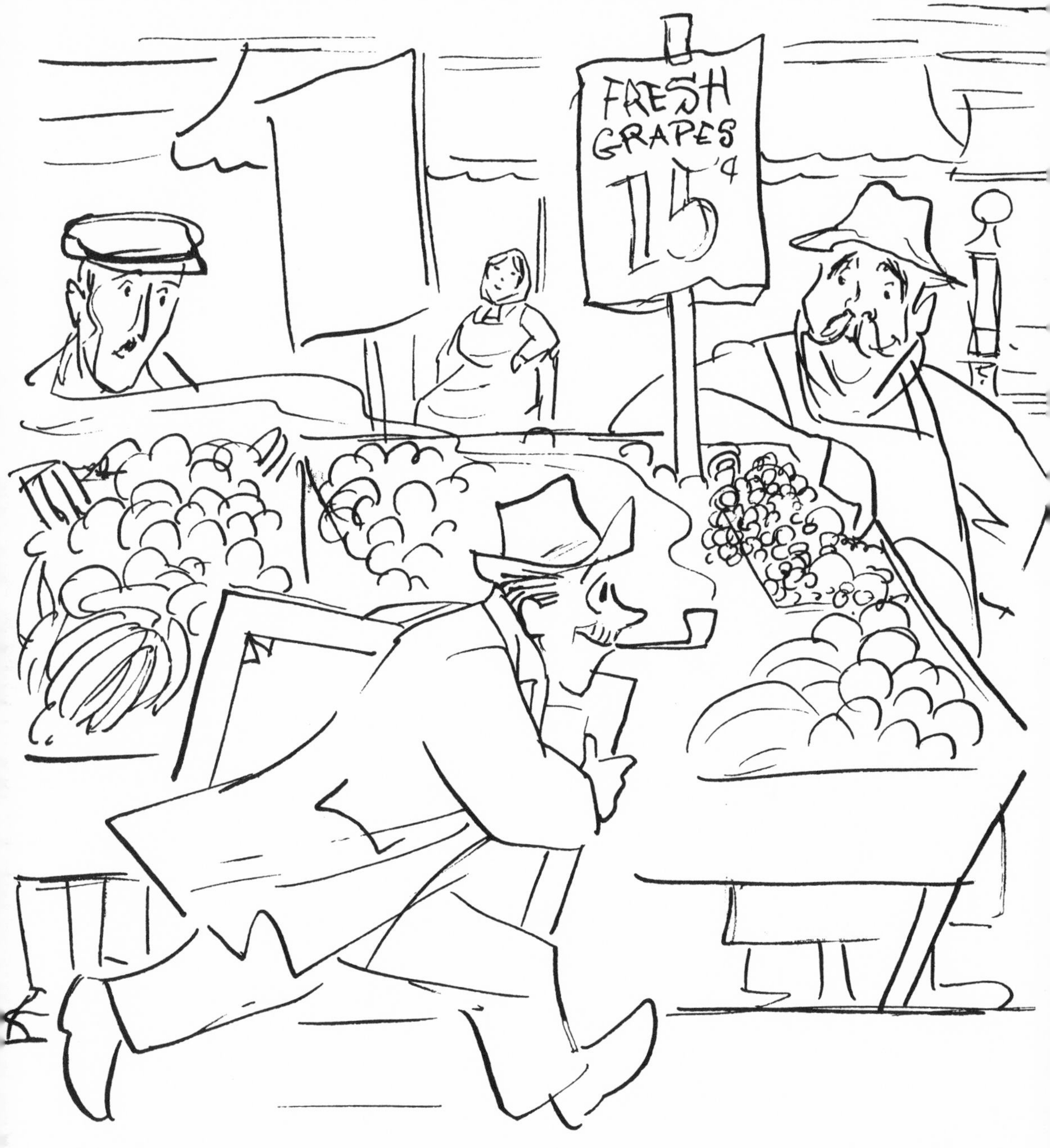
FRESH
GRAPES
15¢

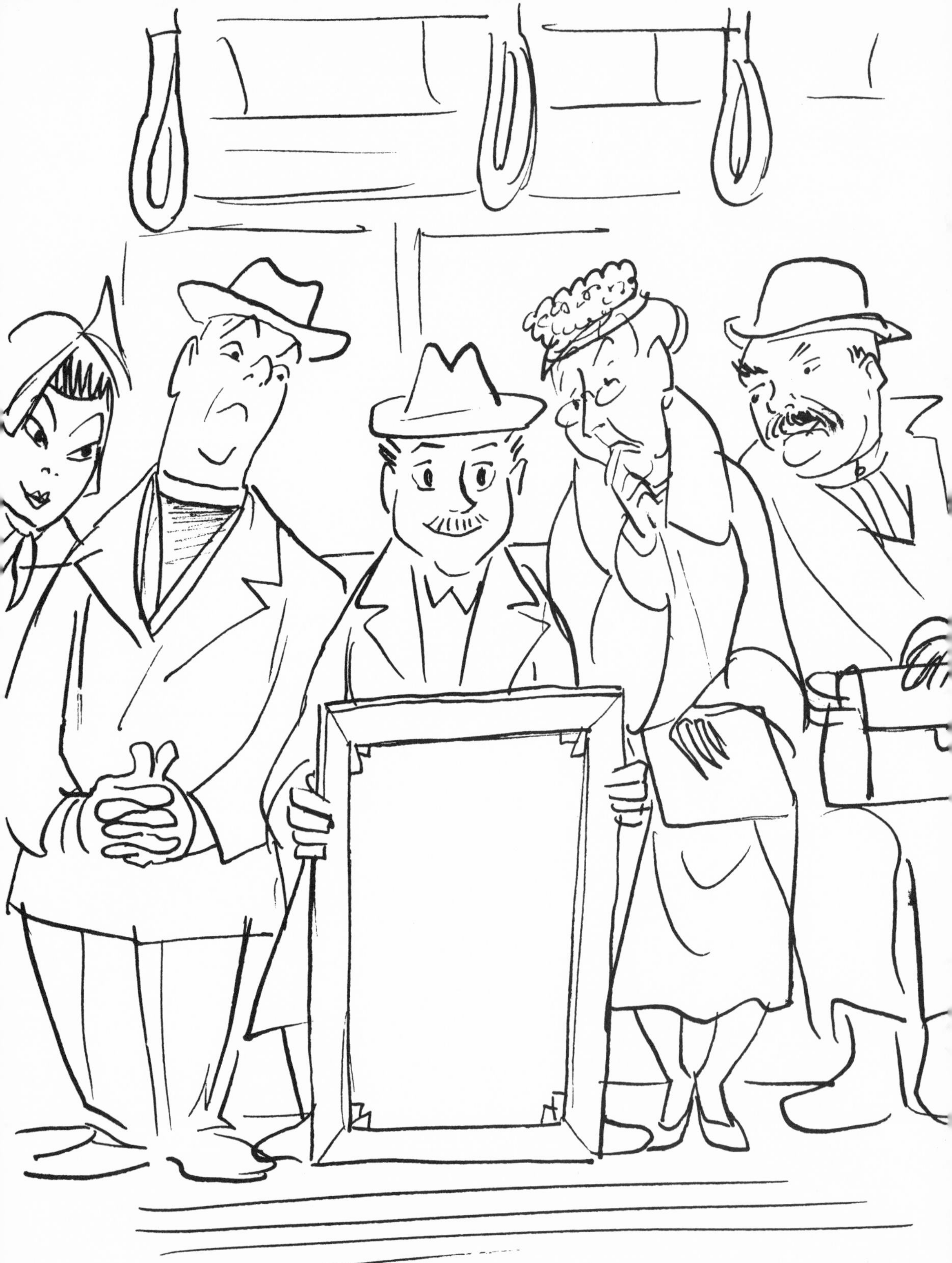

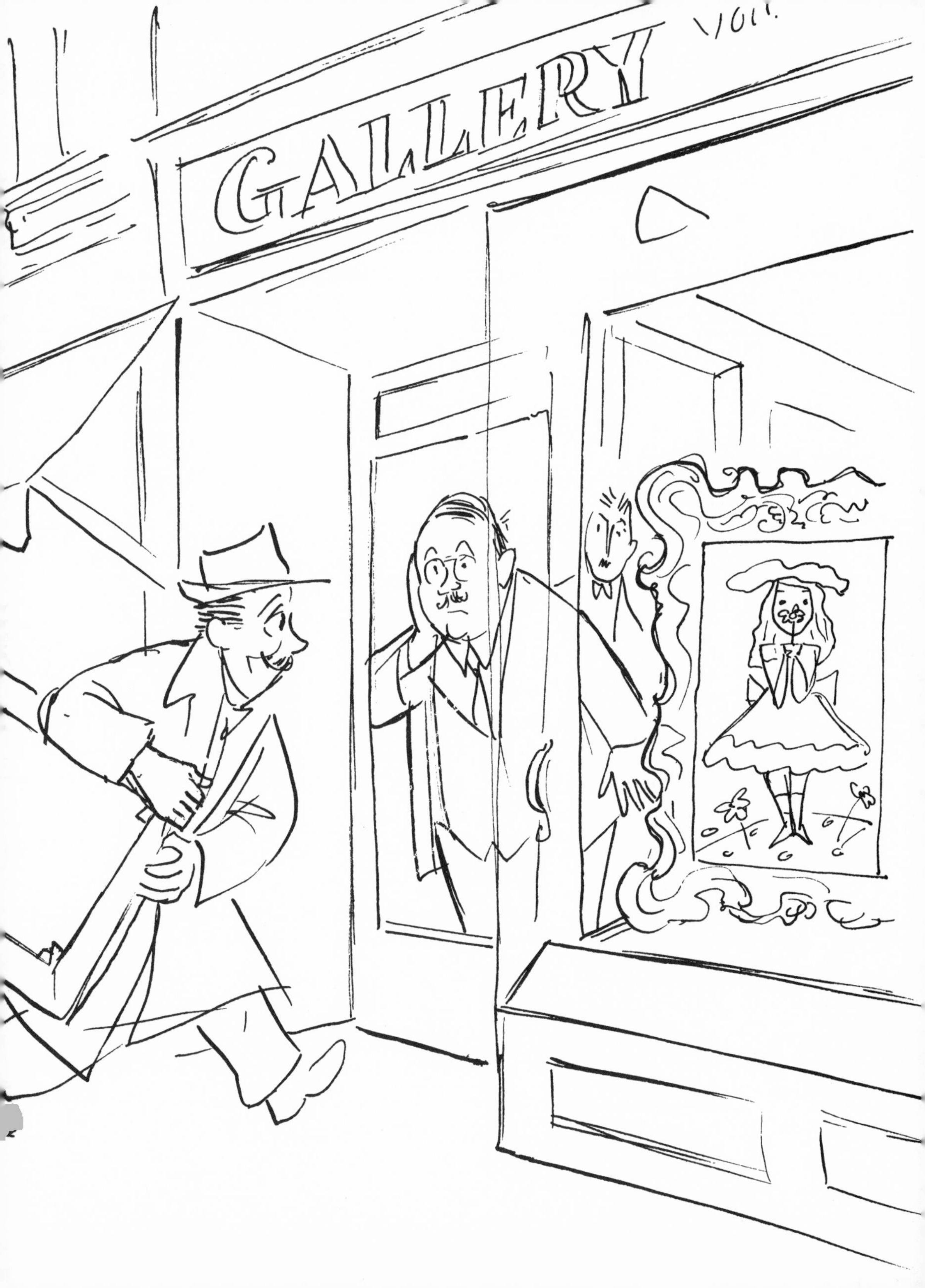
GALLERY

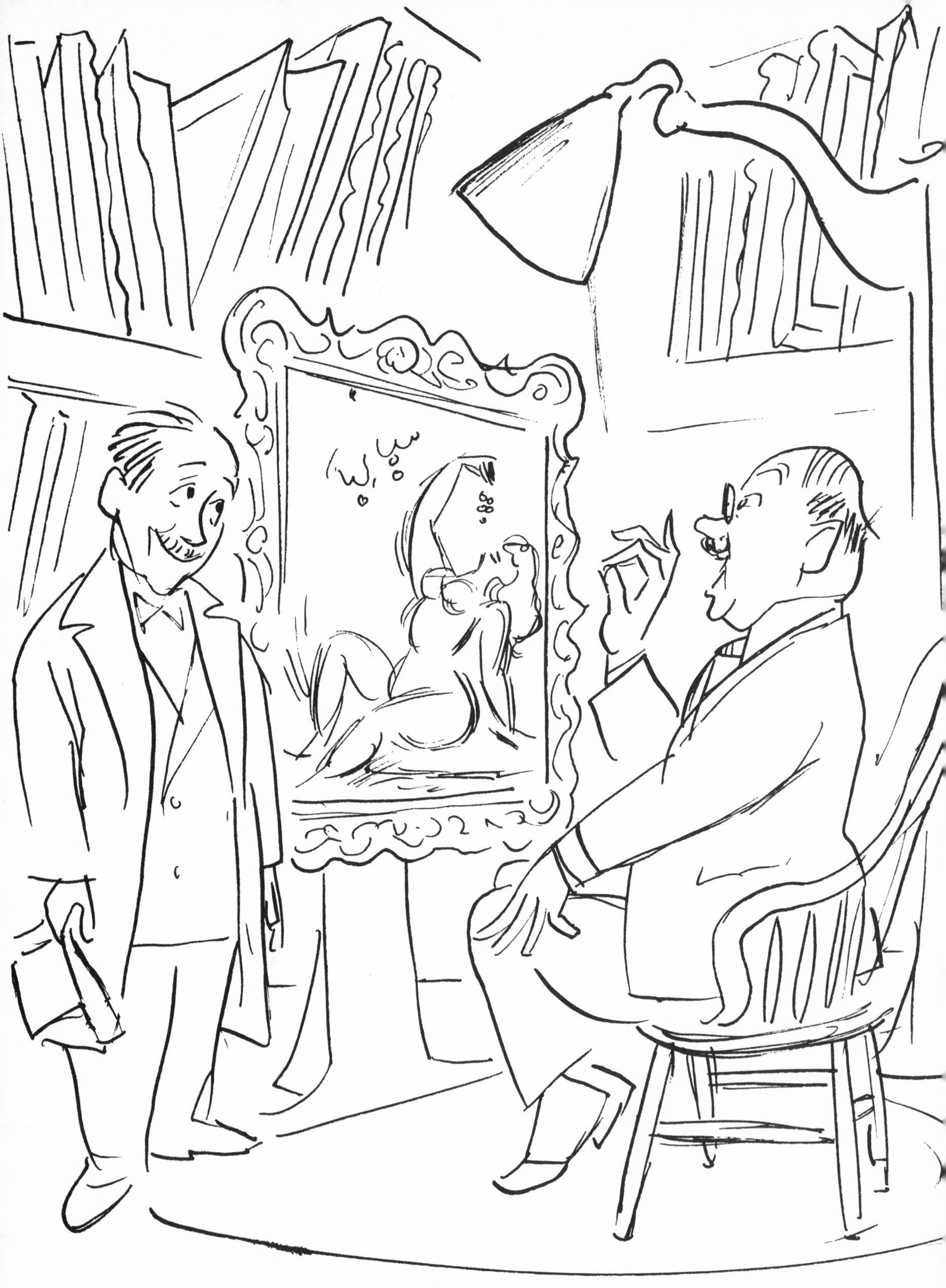

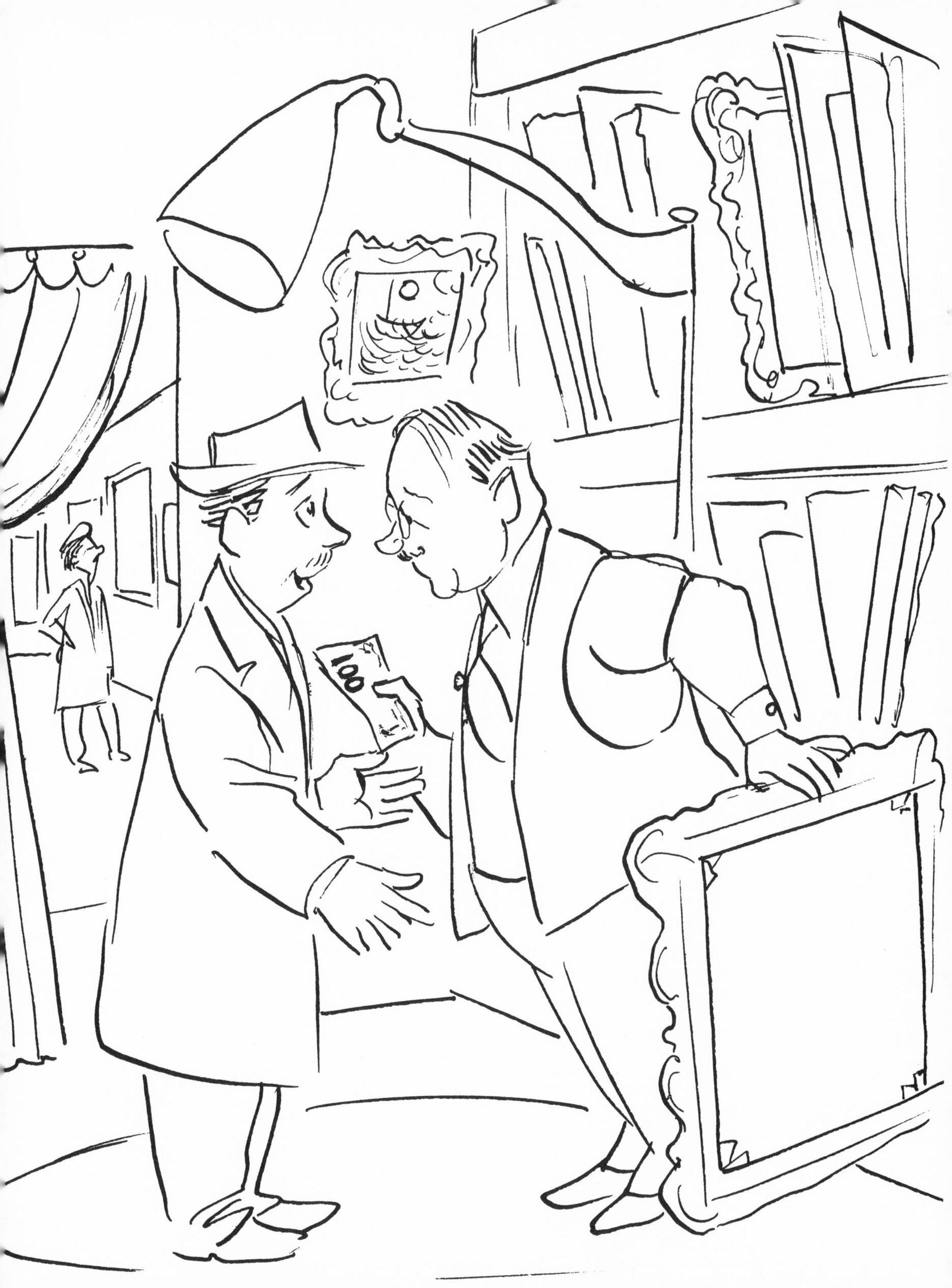
100

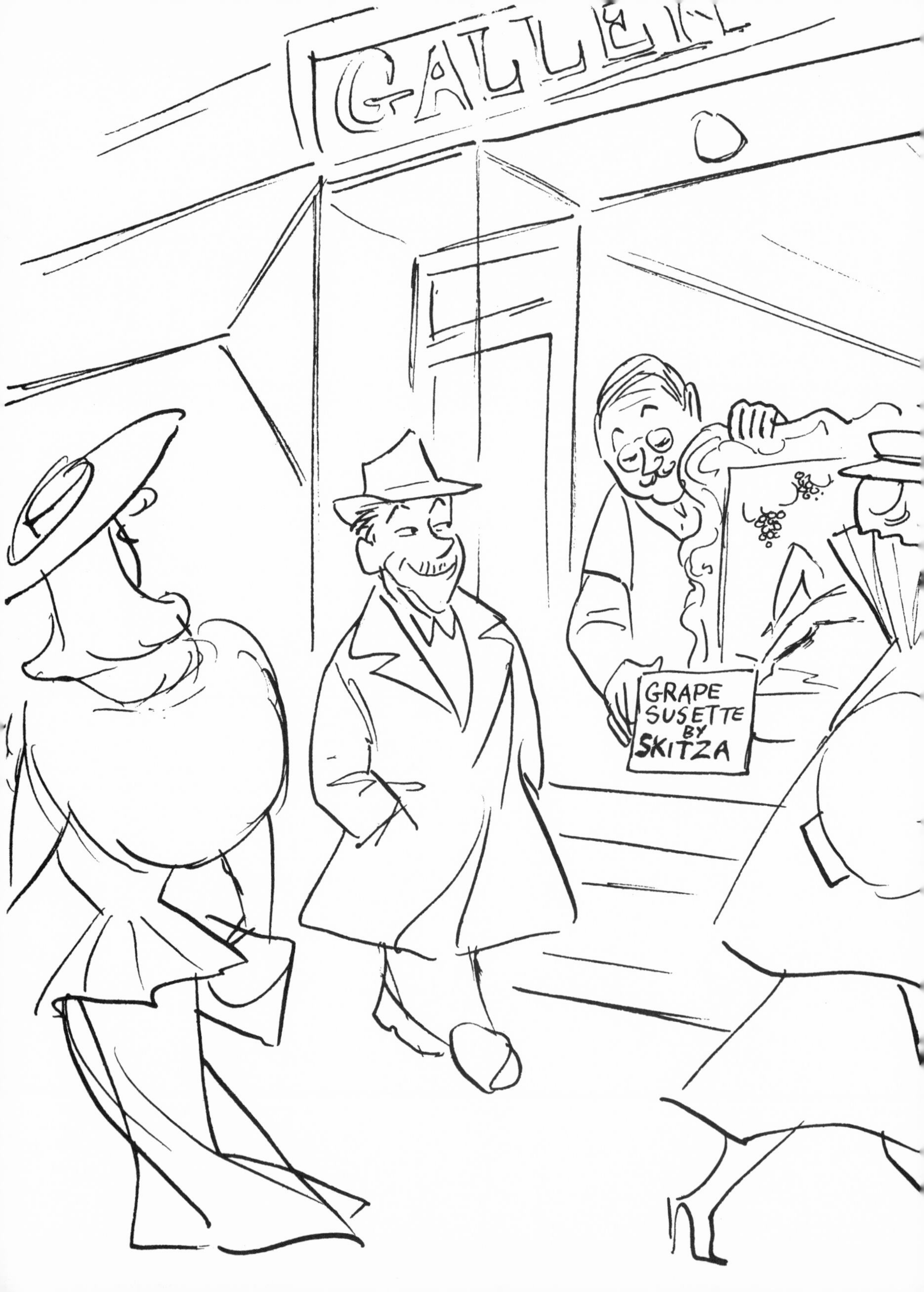
GALLER
GRAPE SUSETTE BY SKITZA

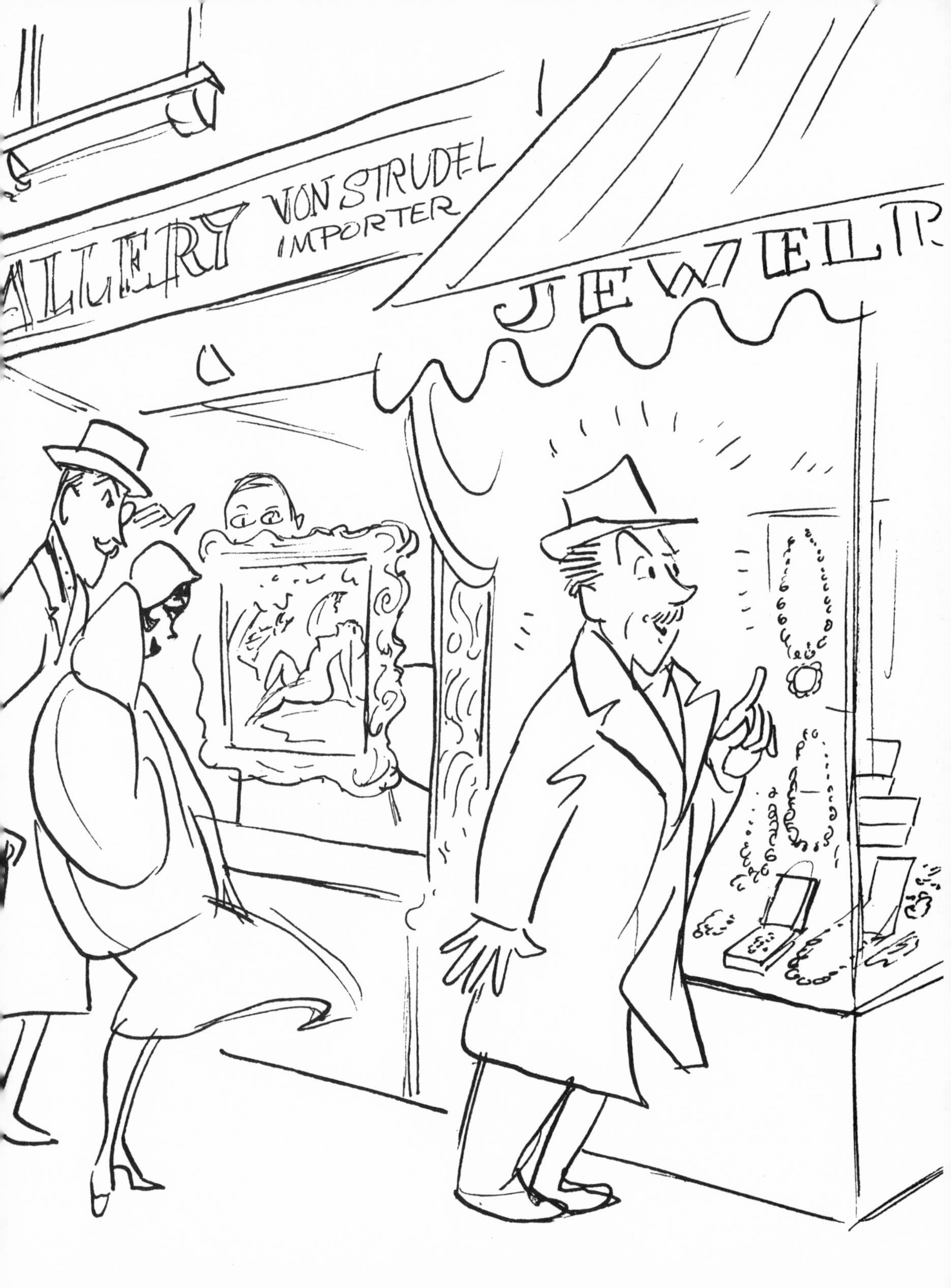
ALLERY
VON STRUDEL
IMPORTER
JEWELR

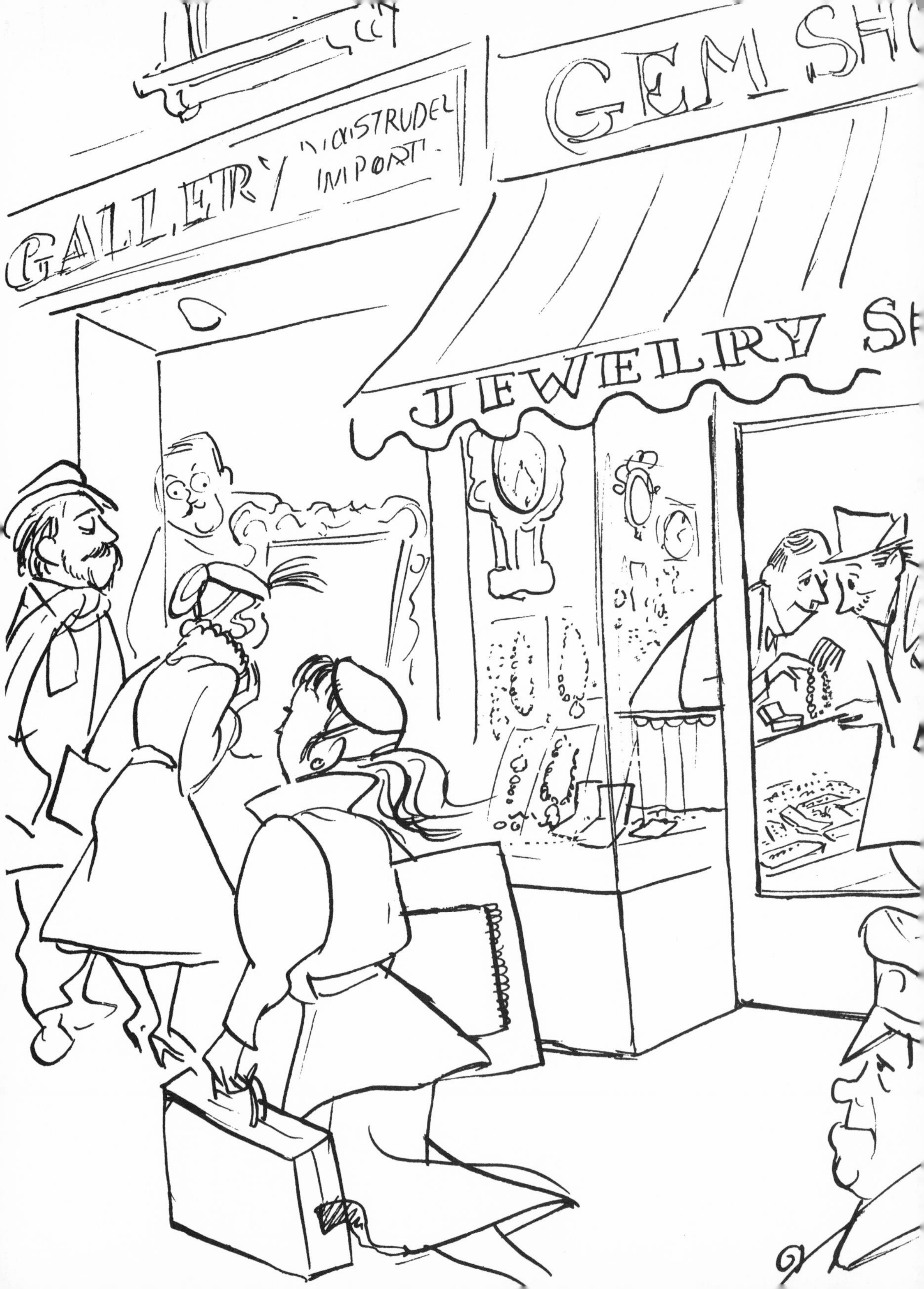
GALLERY
STRUDEL
IMPORT
GEM SH
JEWELRY SH

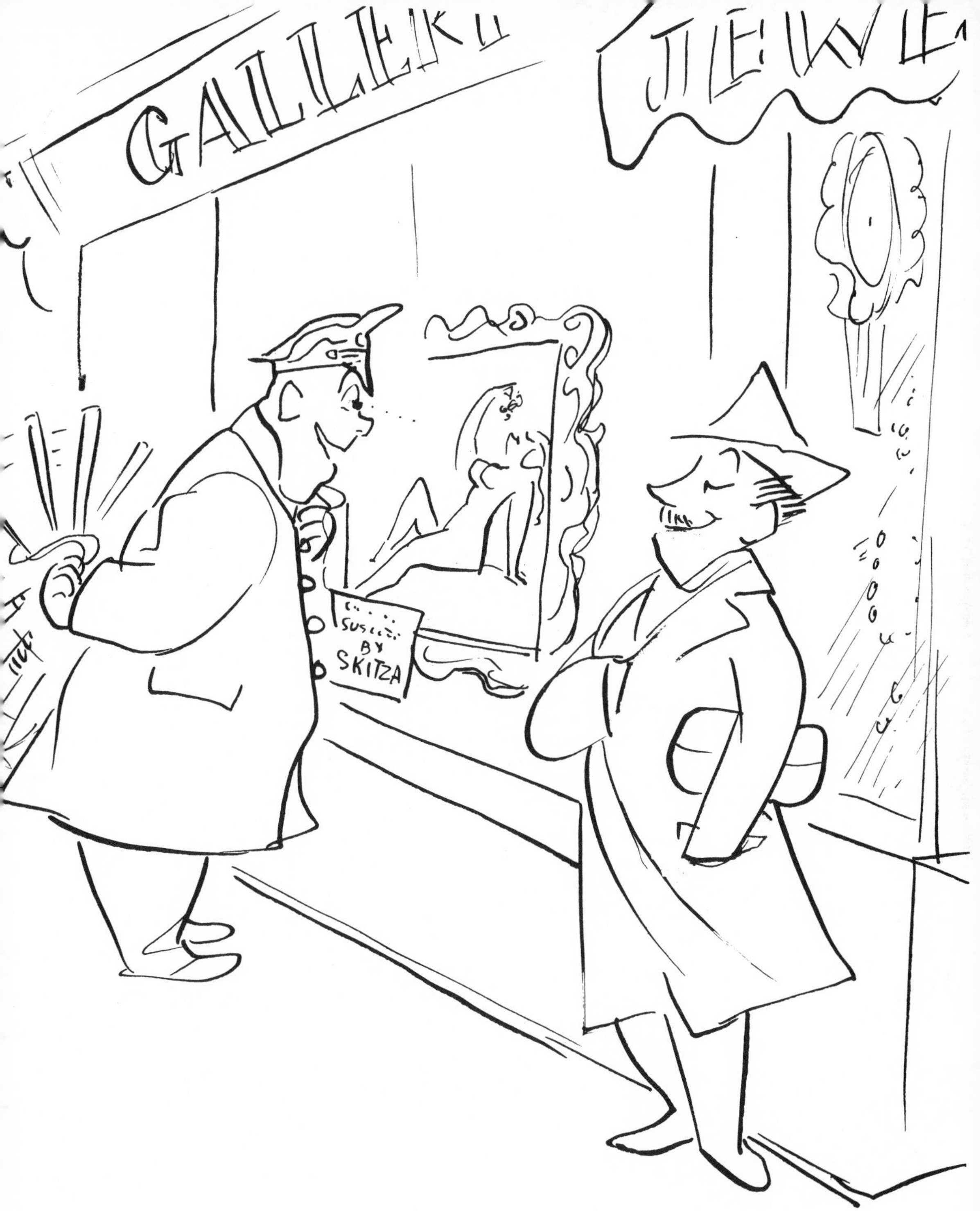

GALLER
JEWE
BY
SKITZA

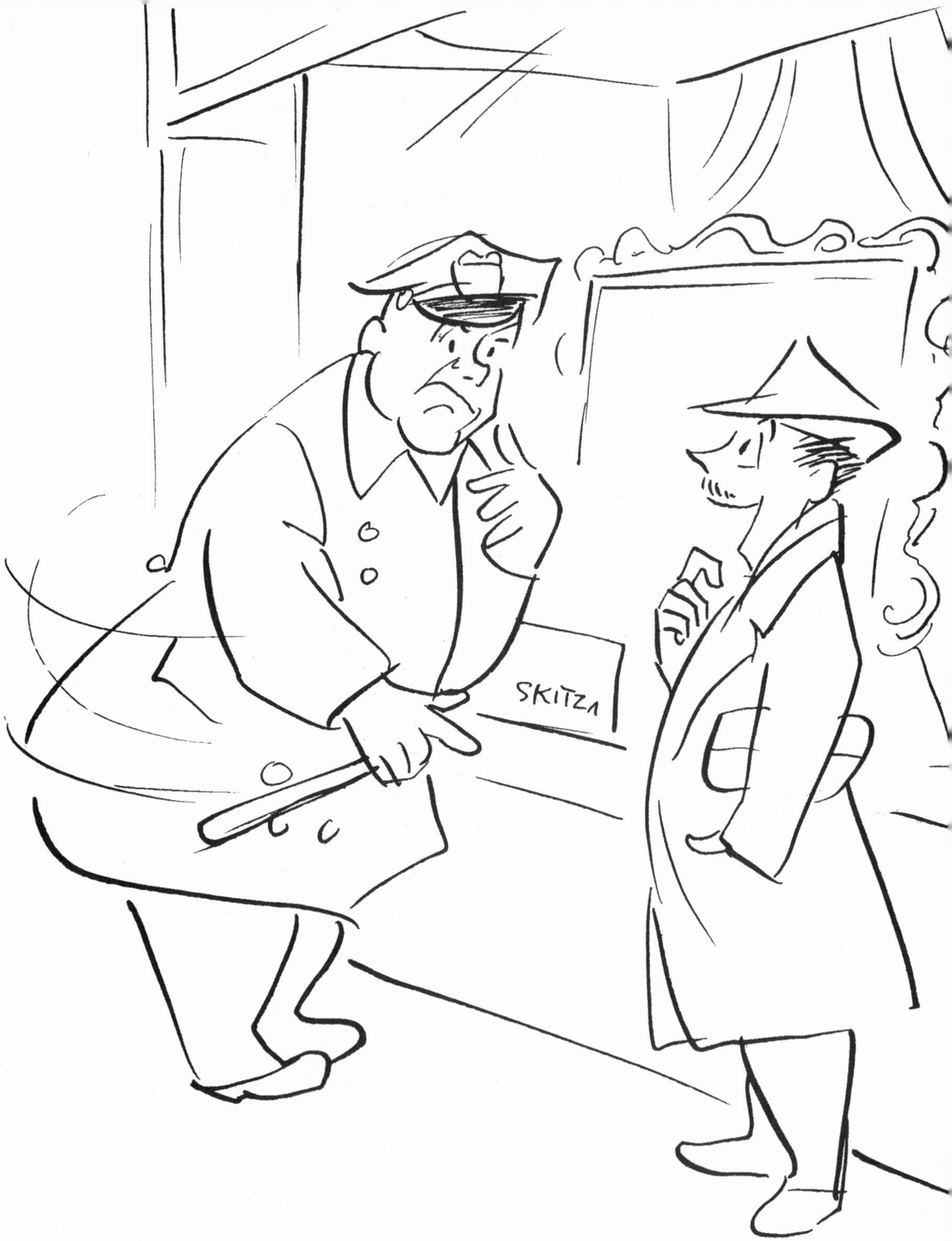
SKITZ1

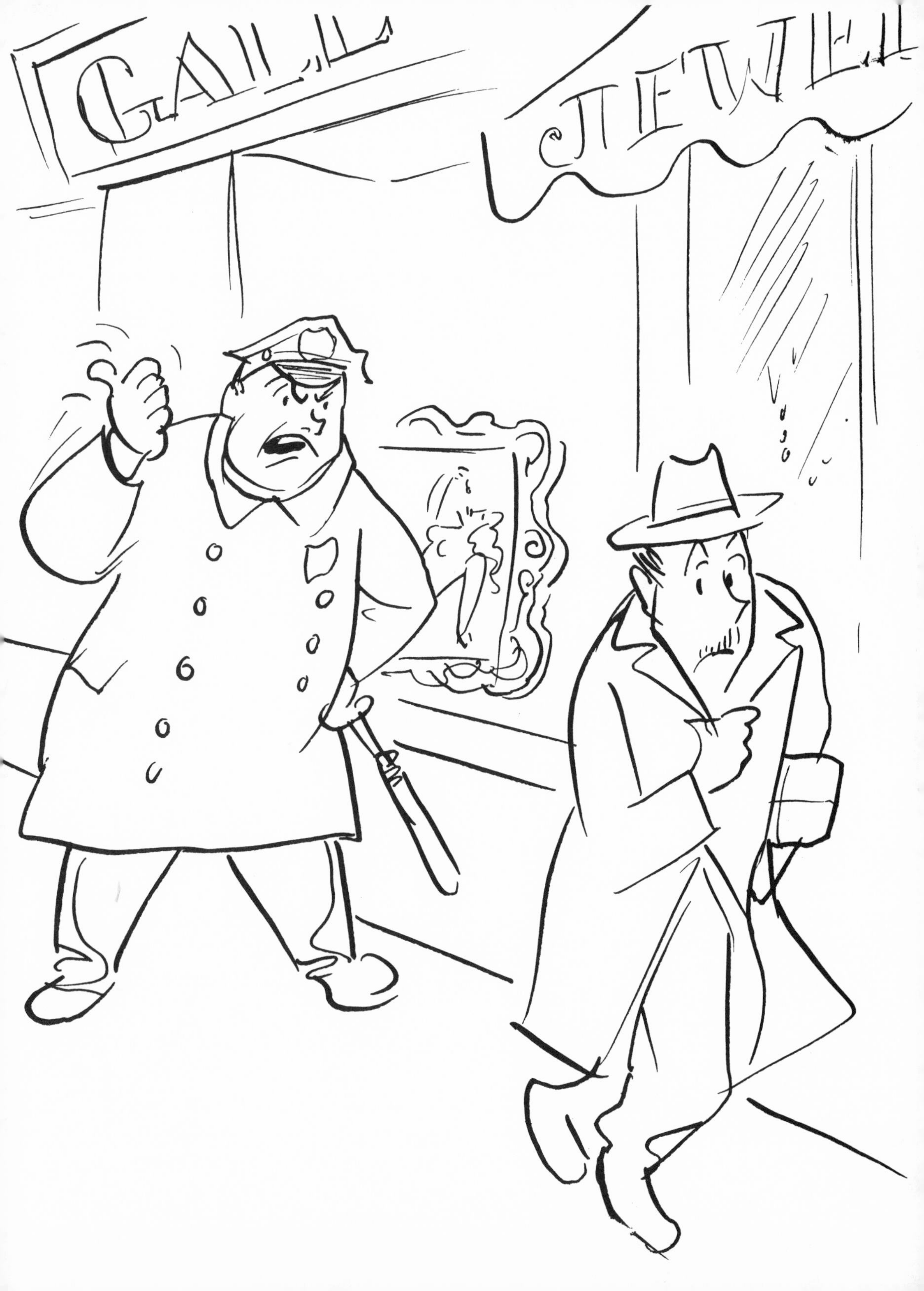
GALL
JEWEL

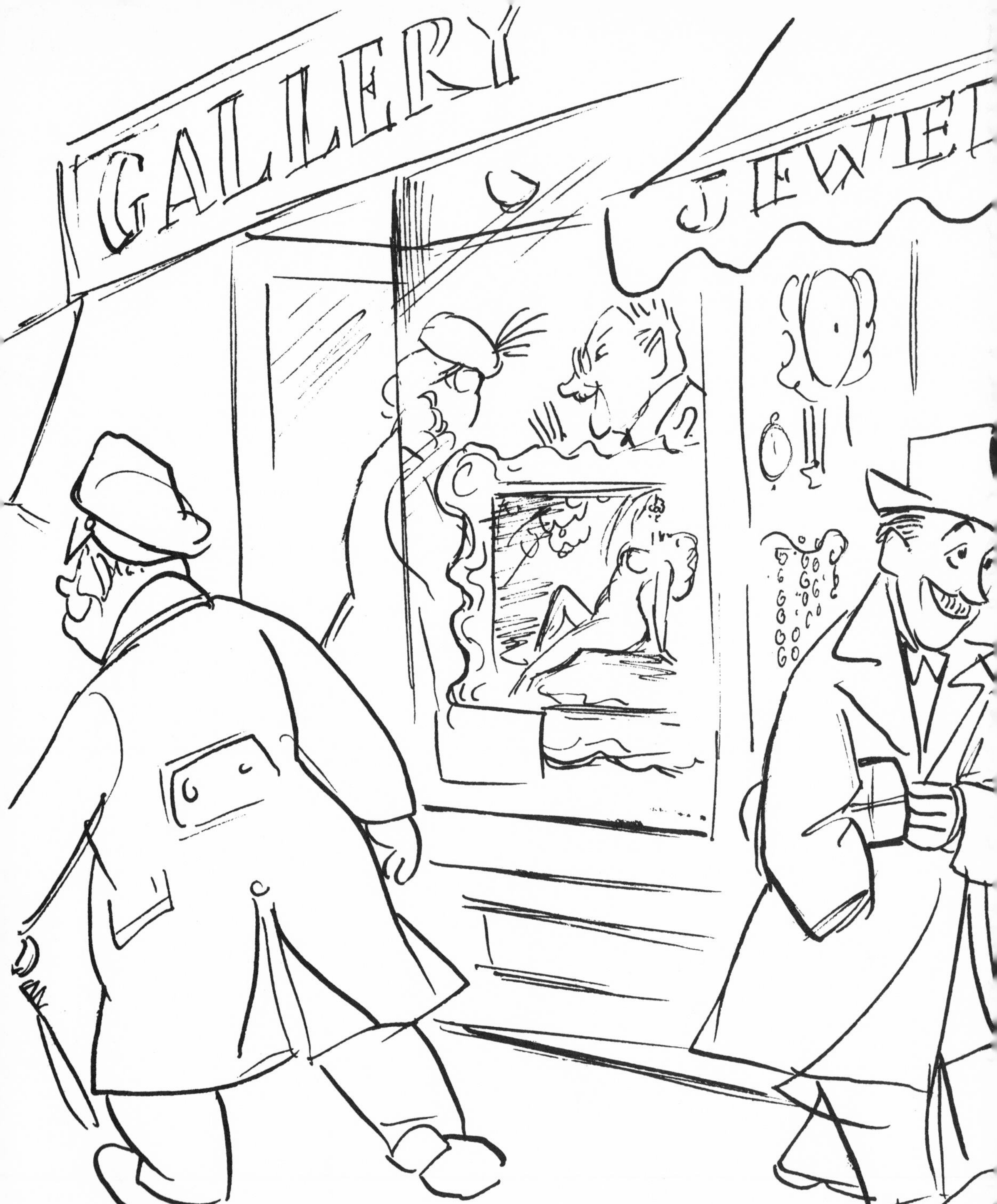
GALLERY

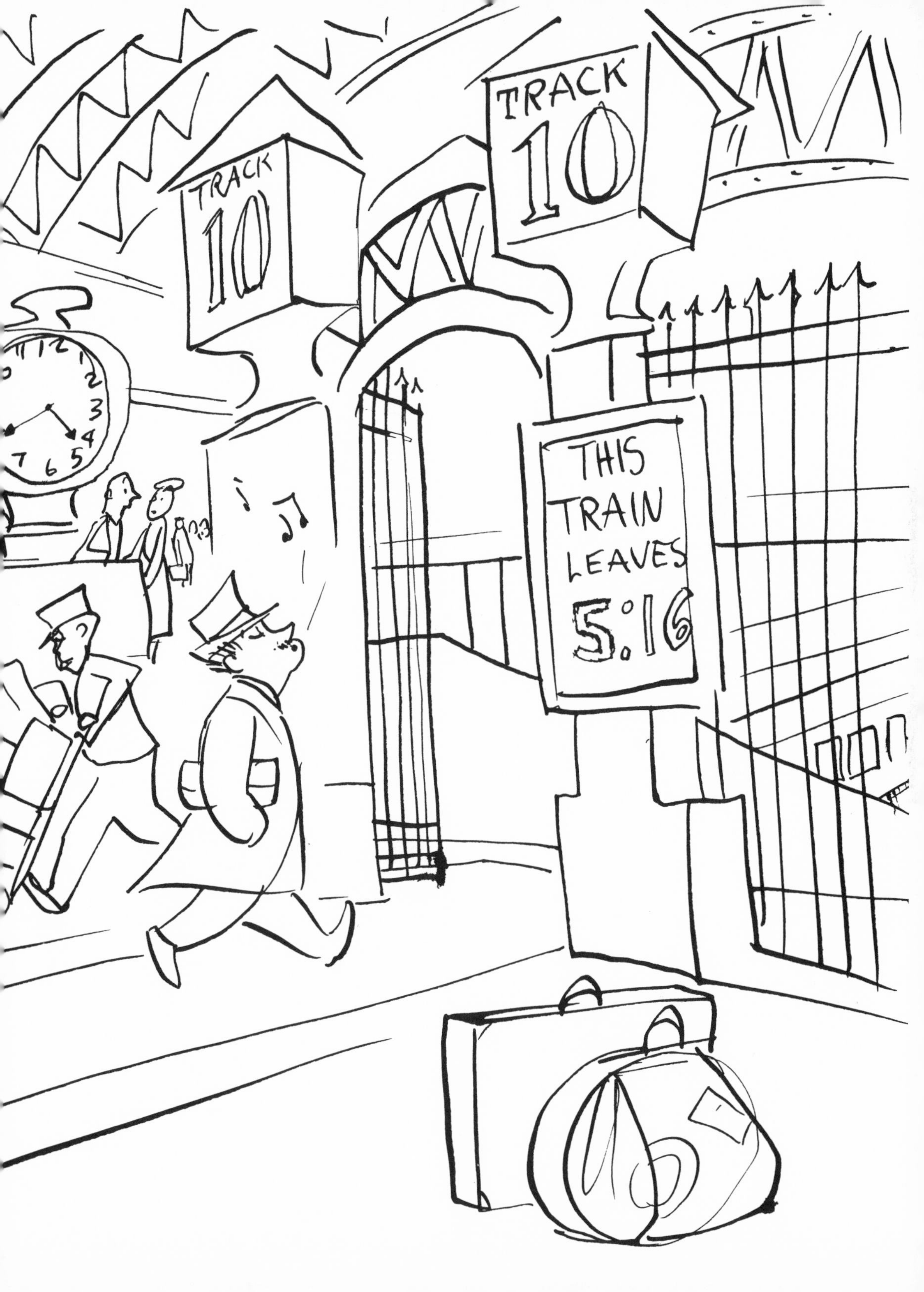
TRACK 10
TRACK 10
THIS TRAIN LEAVES 5:16

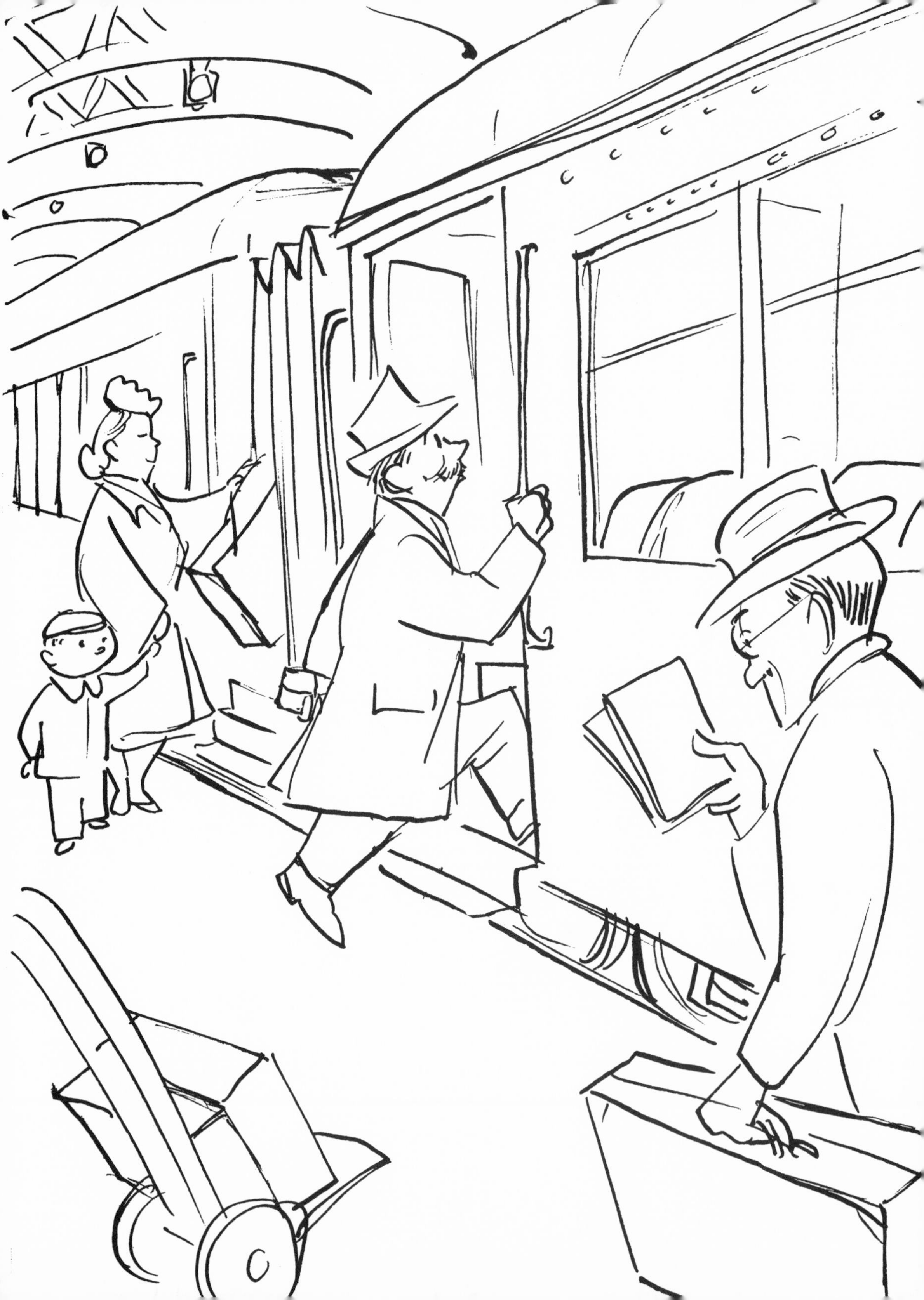

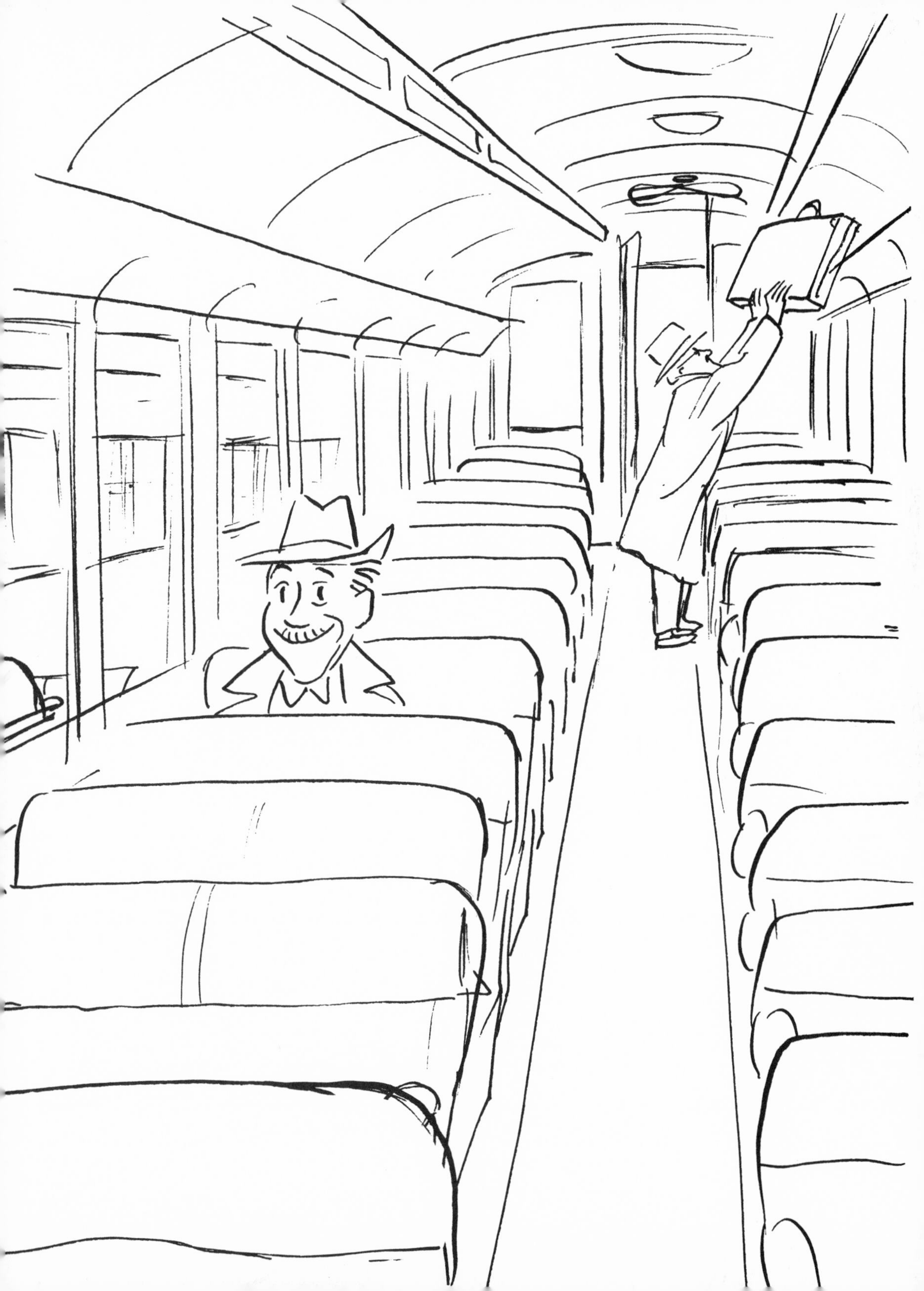

DURING ALL THIS TIME
IN ANOTHER PART
OF THE CITY —

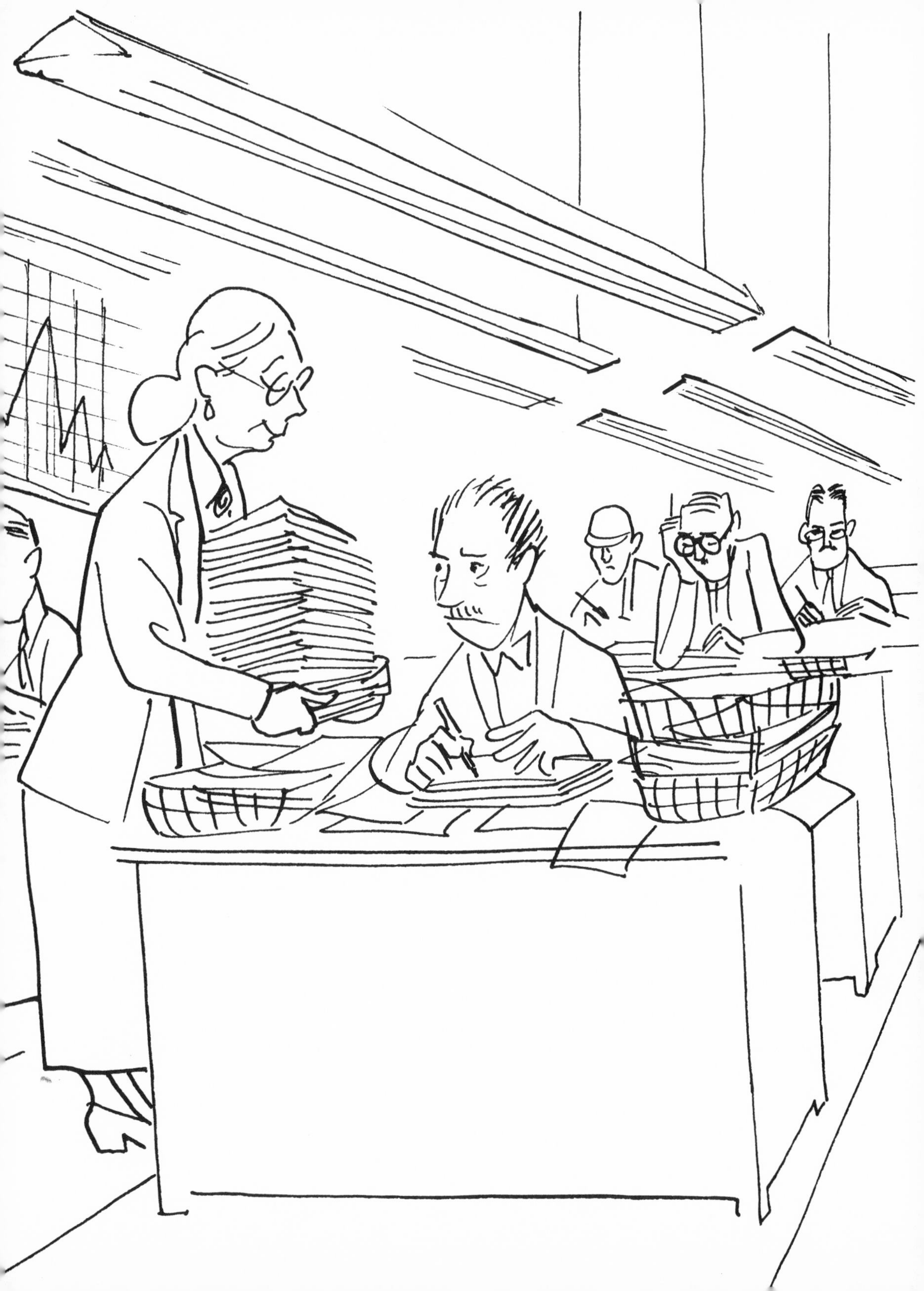

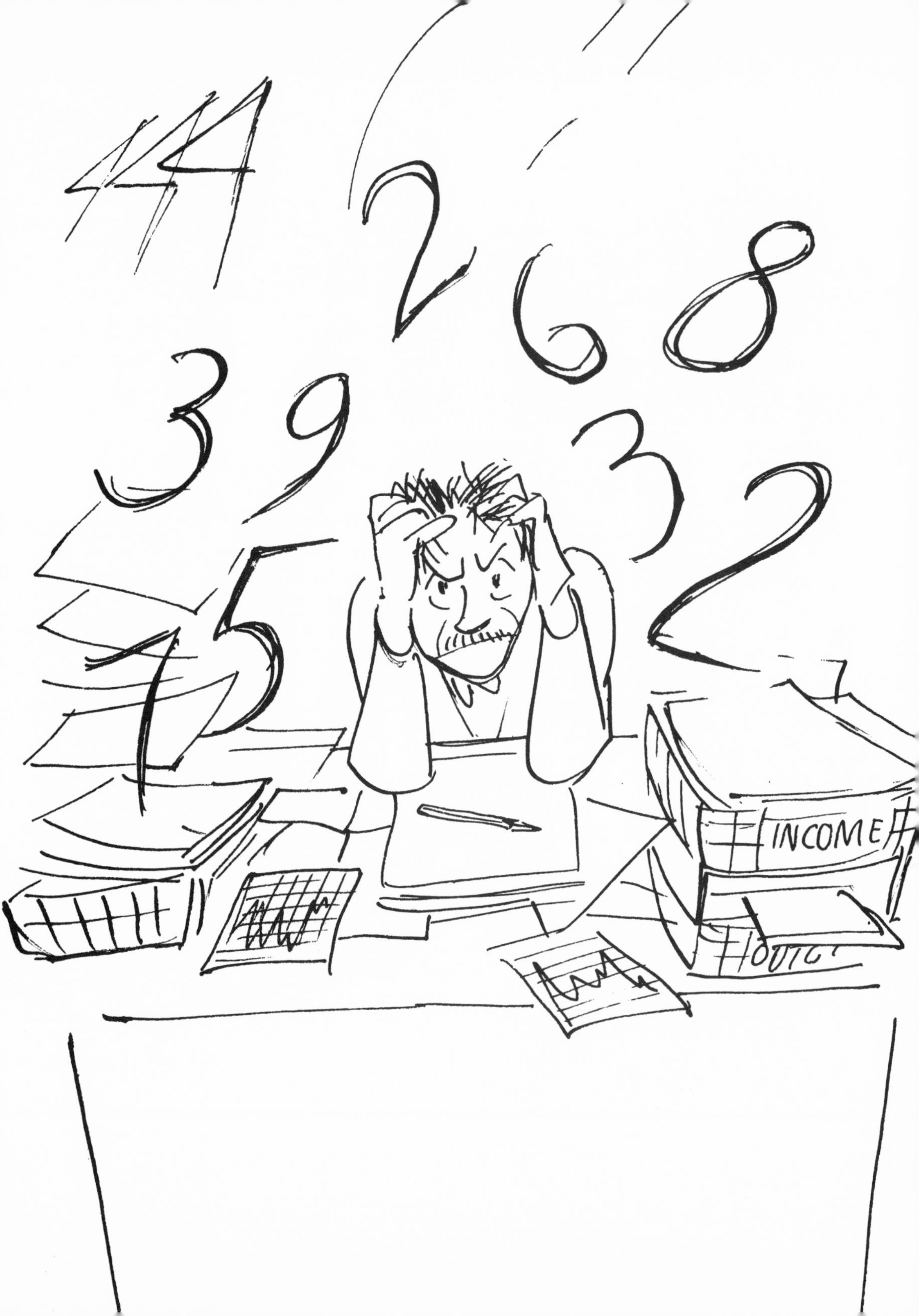
INCOME

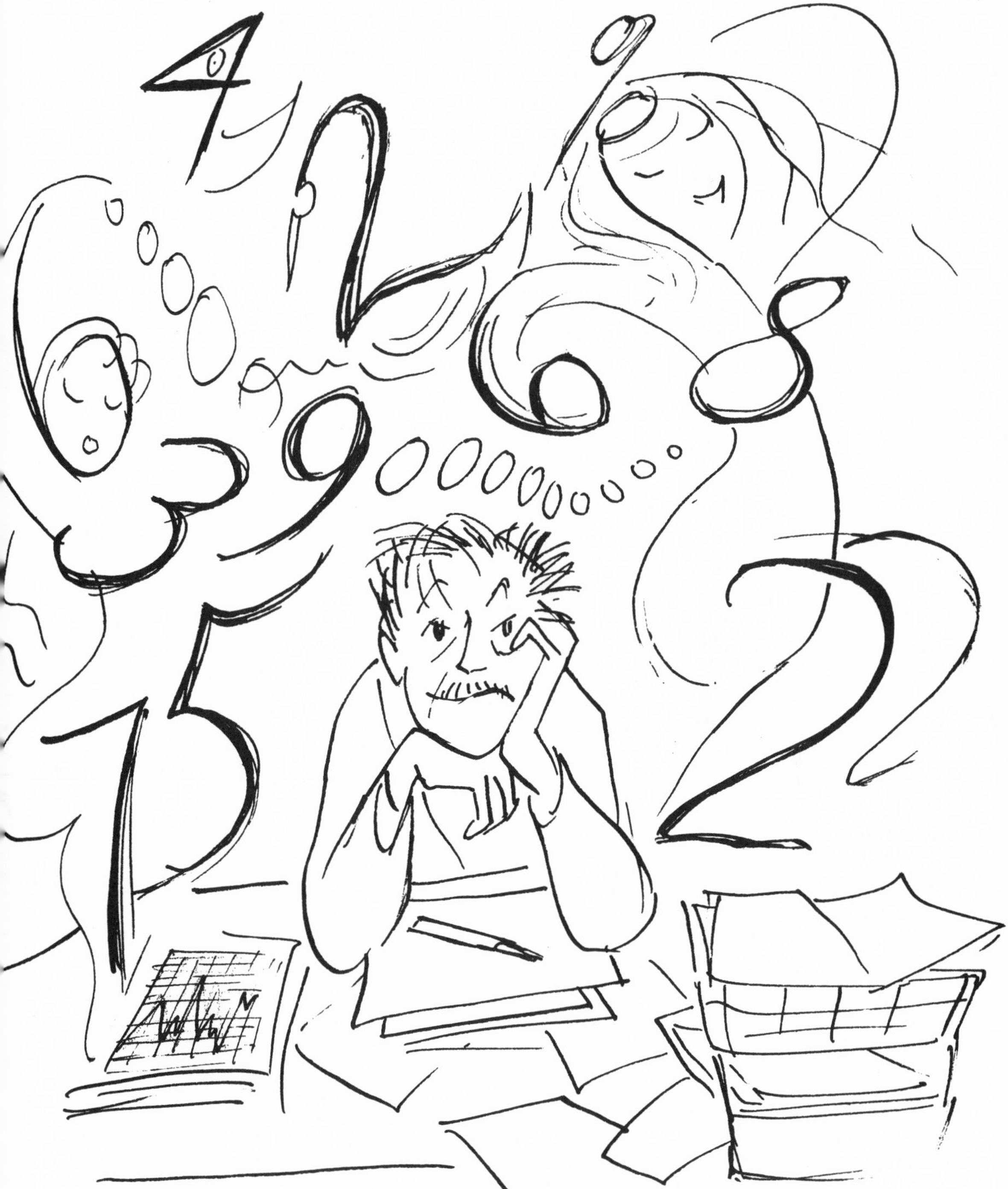

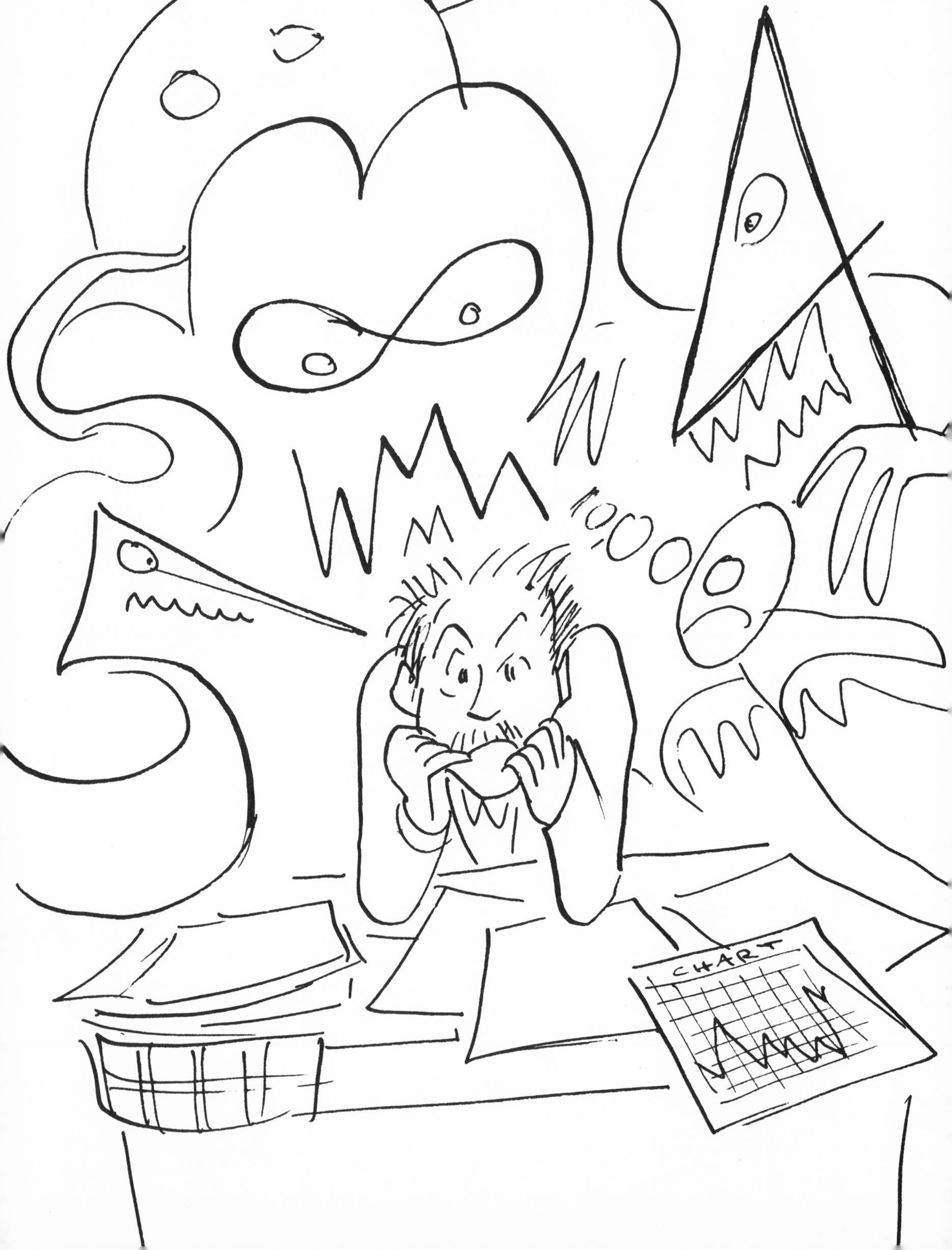
CHART

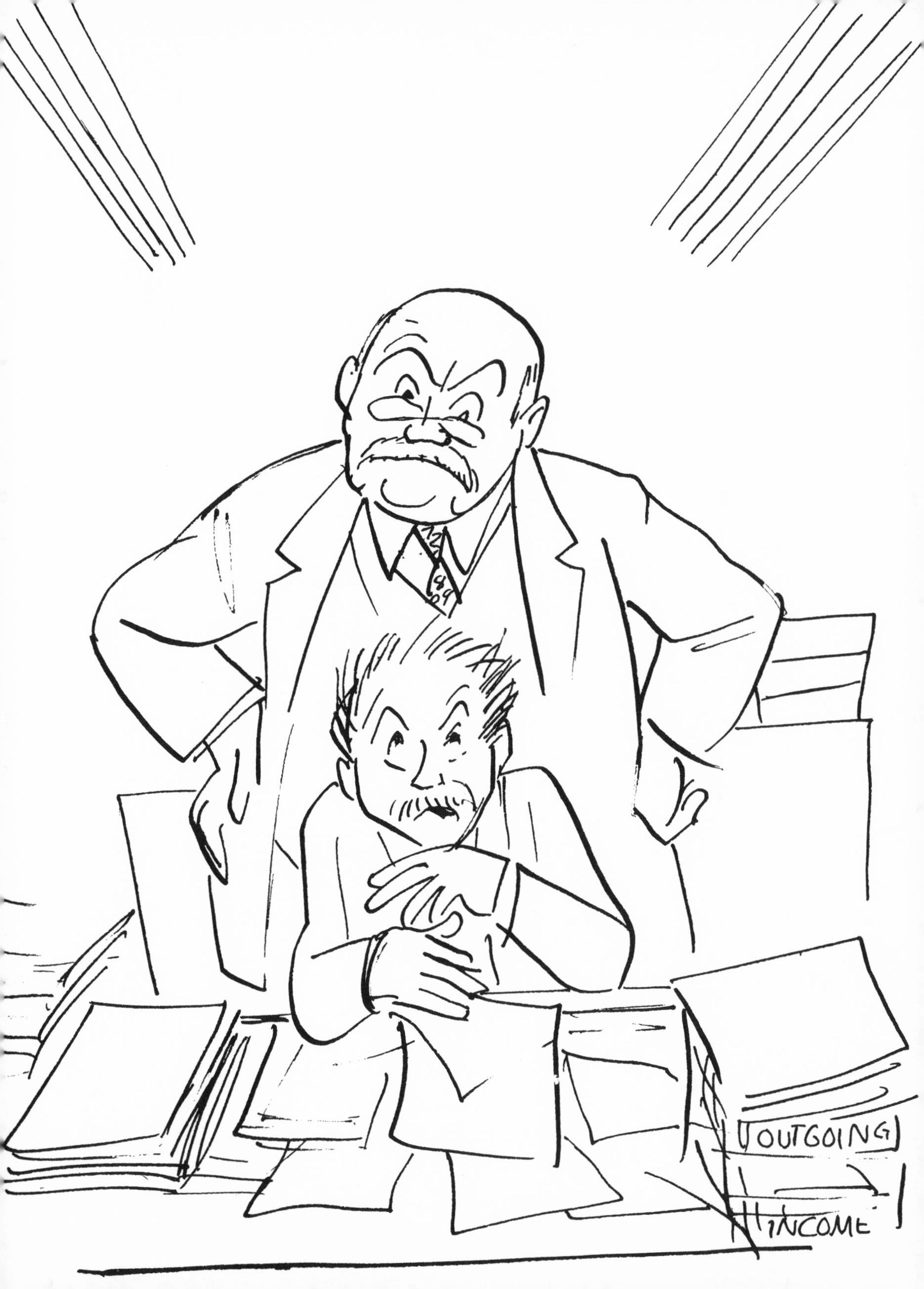
OUTGOING
INCOME

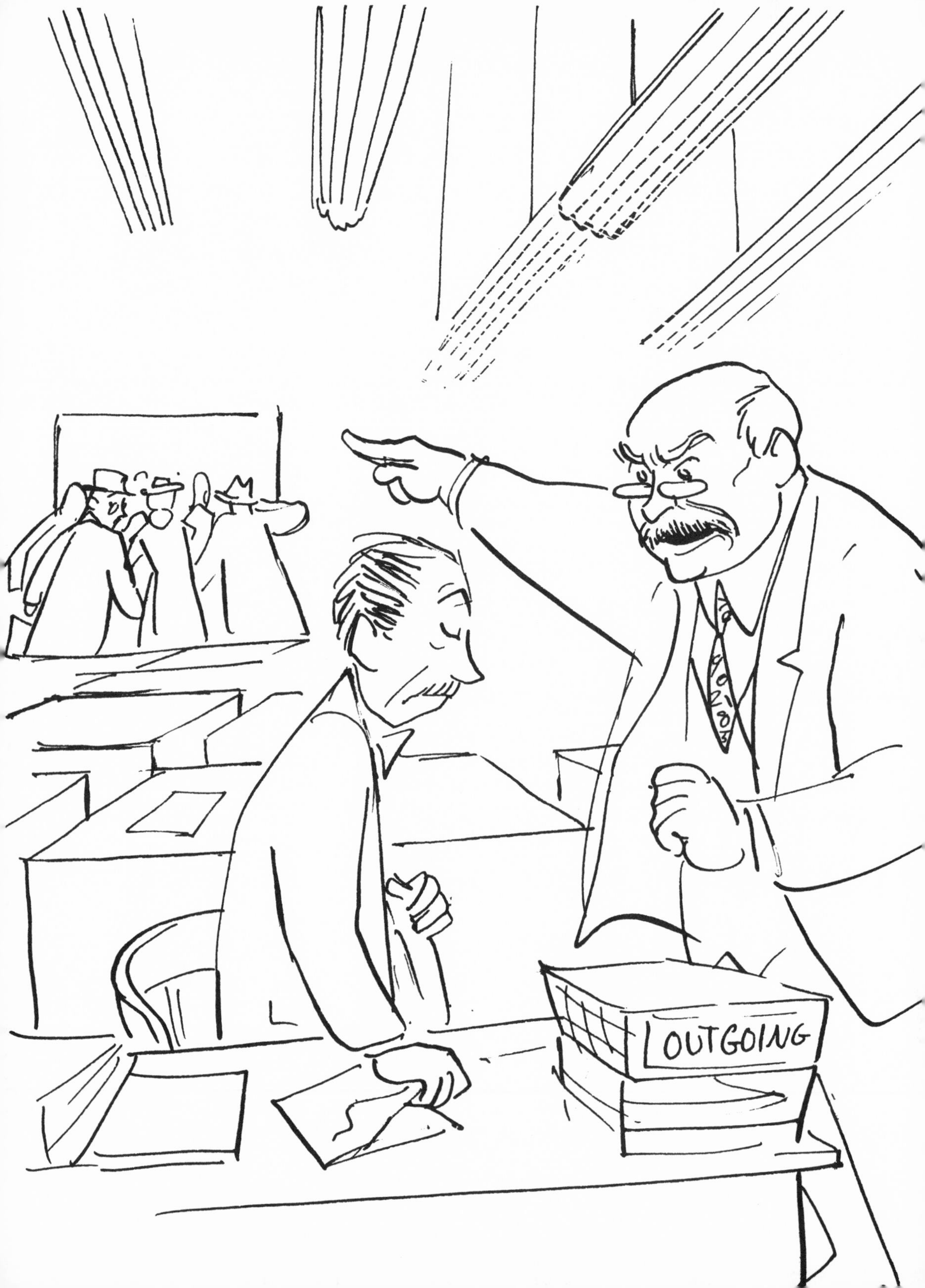
OUTGOING

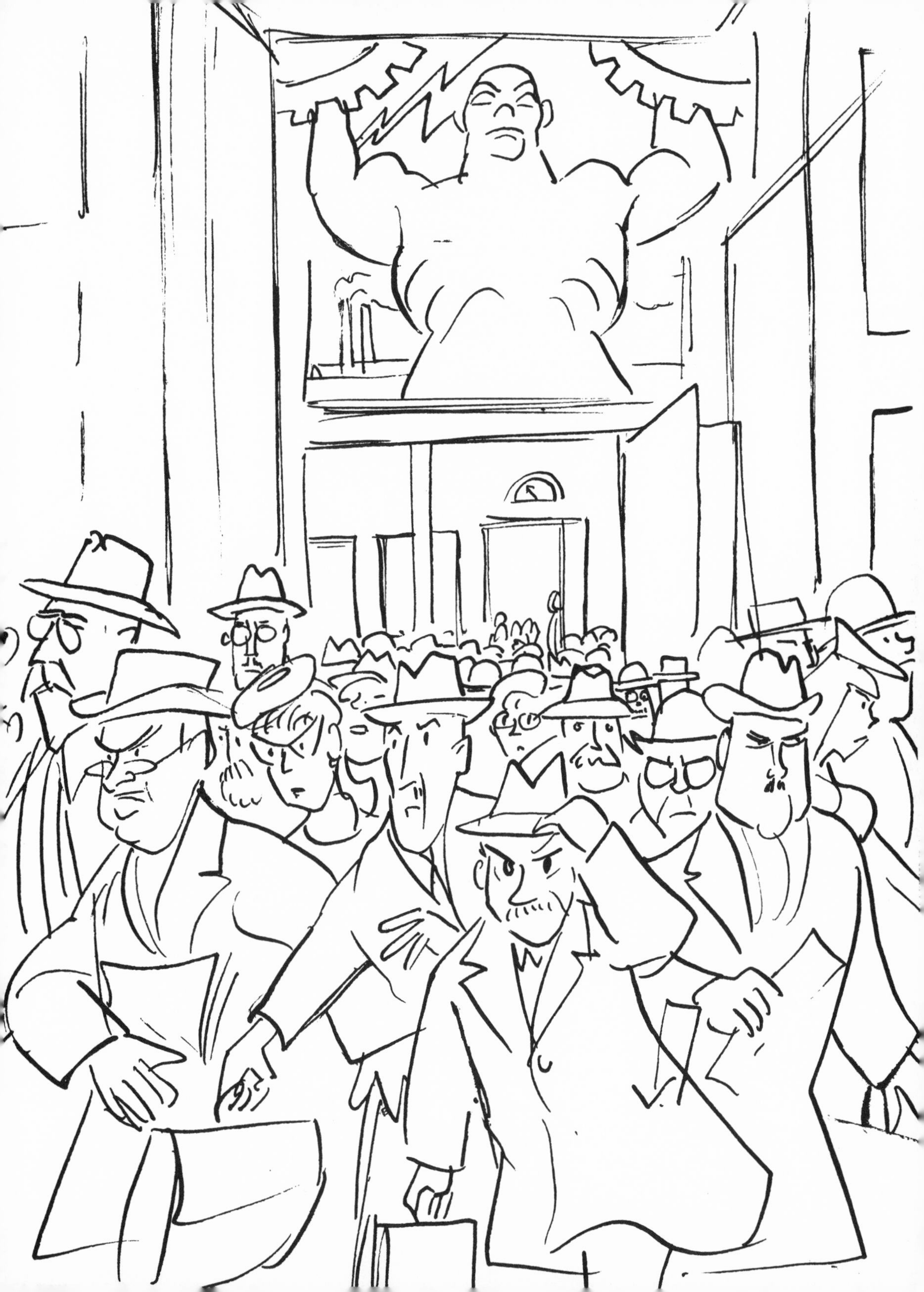

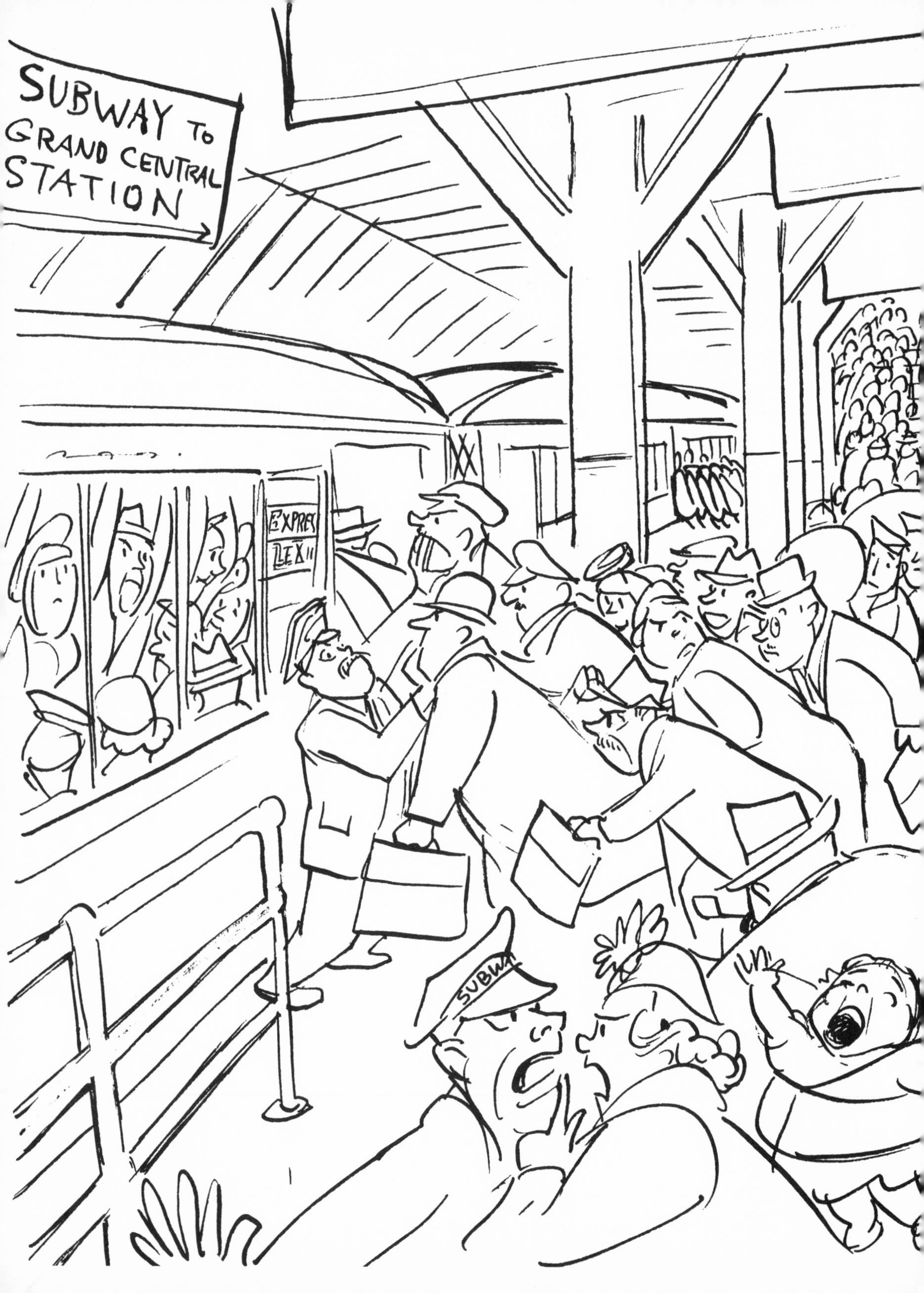

SUBWAY TO
GRAND CENTRAL
STATION
EXPRESS
LEX
SUBWA

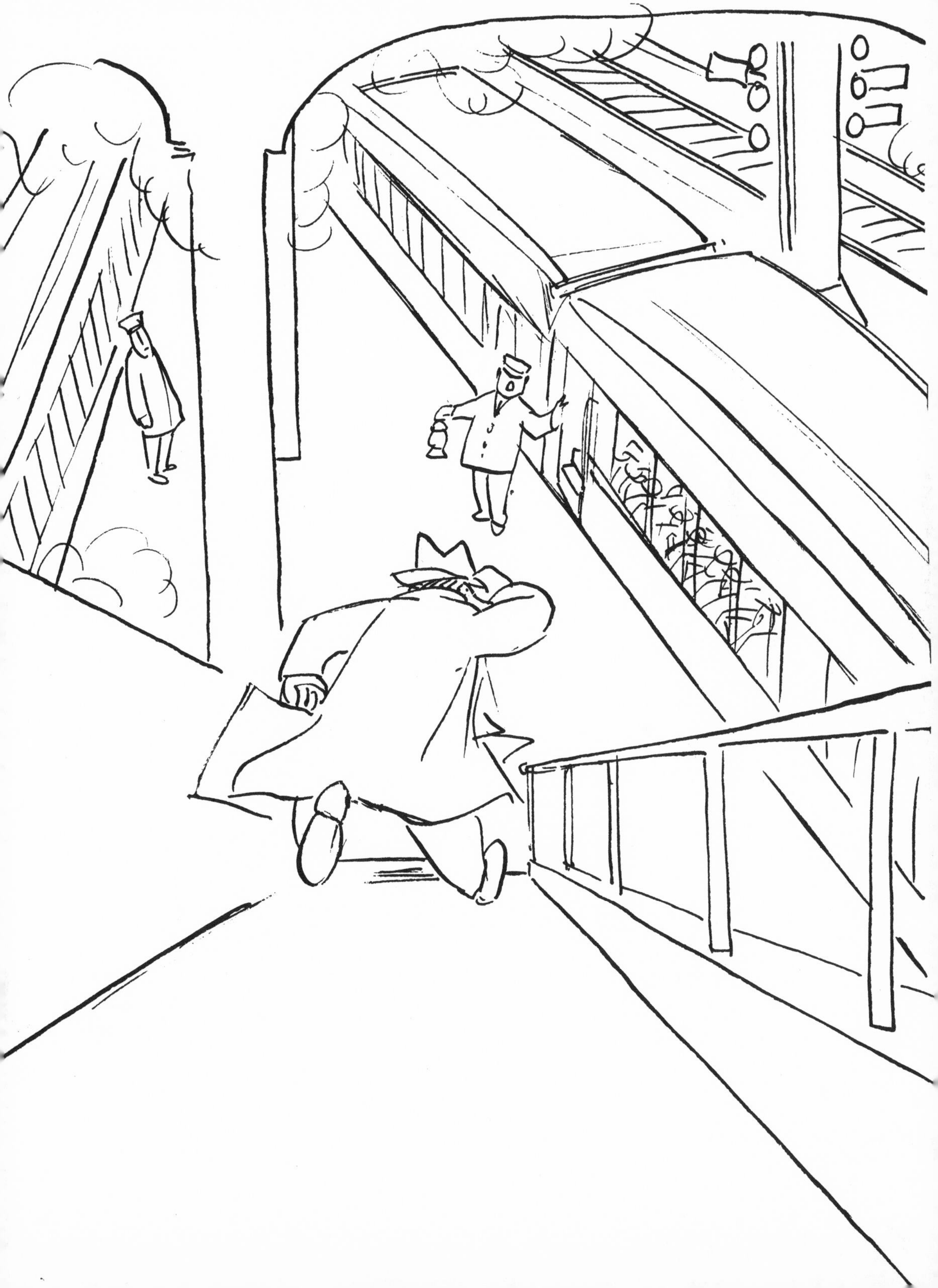

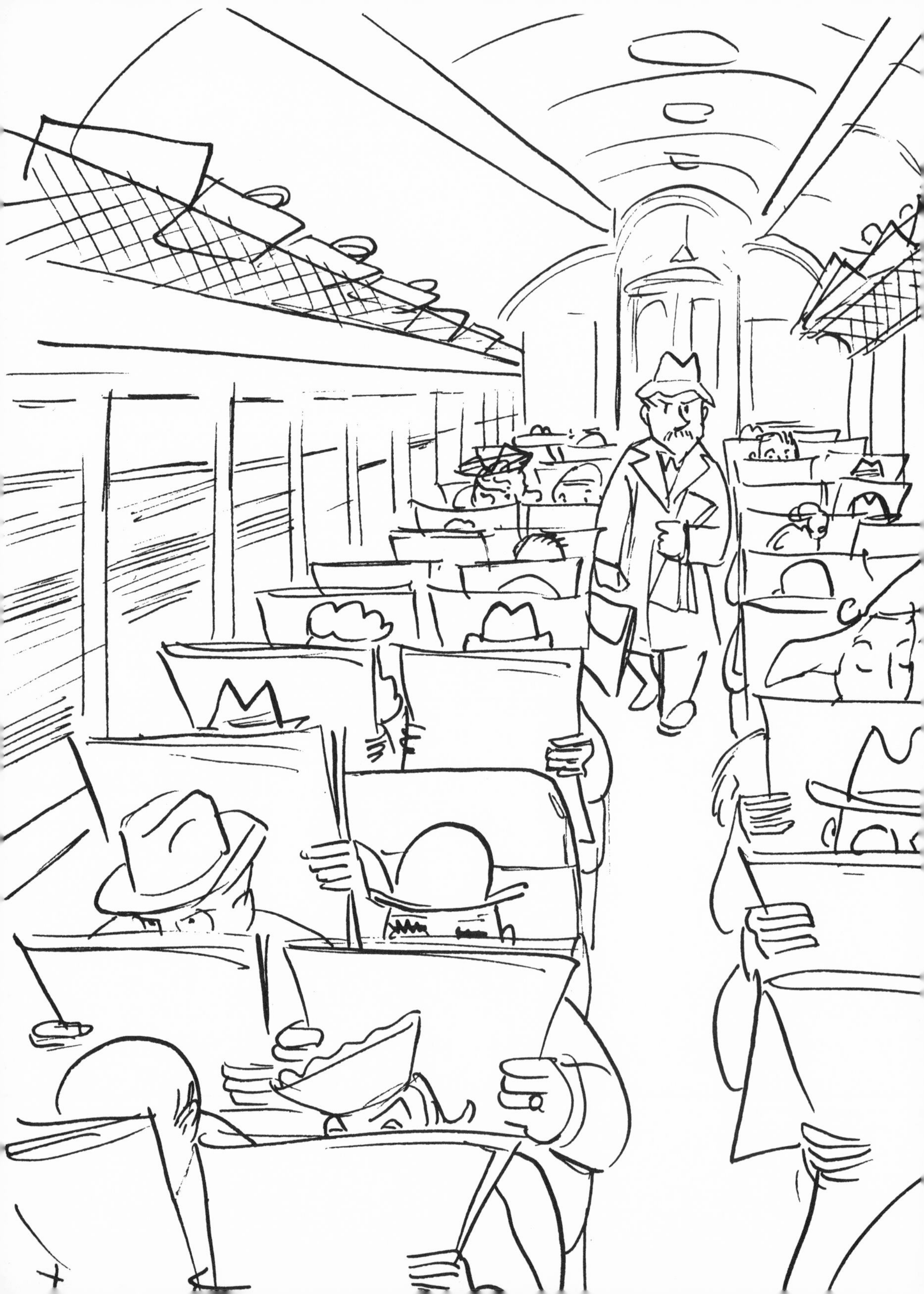

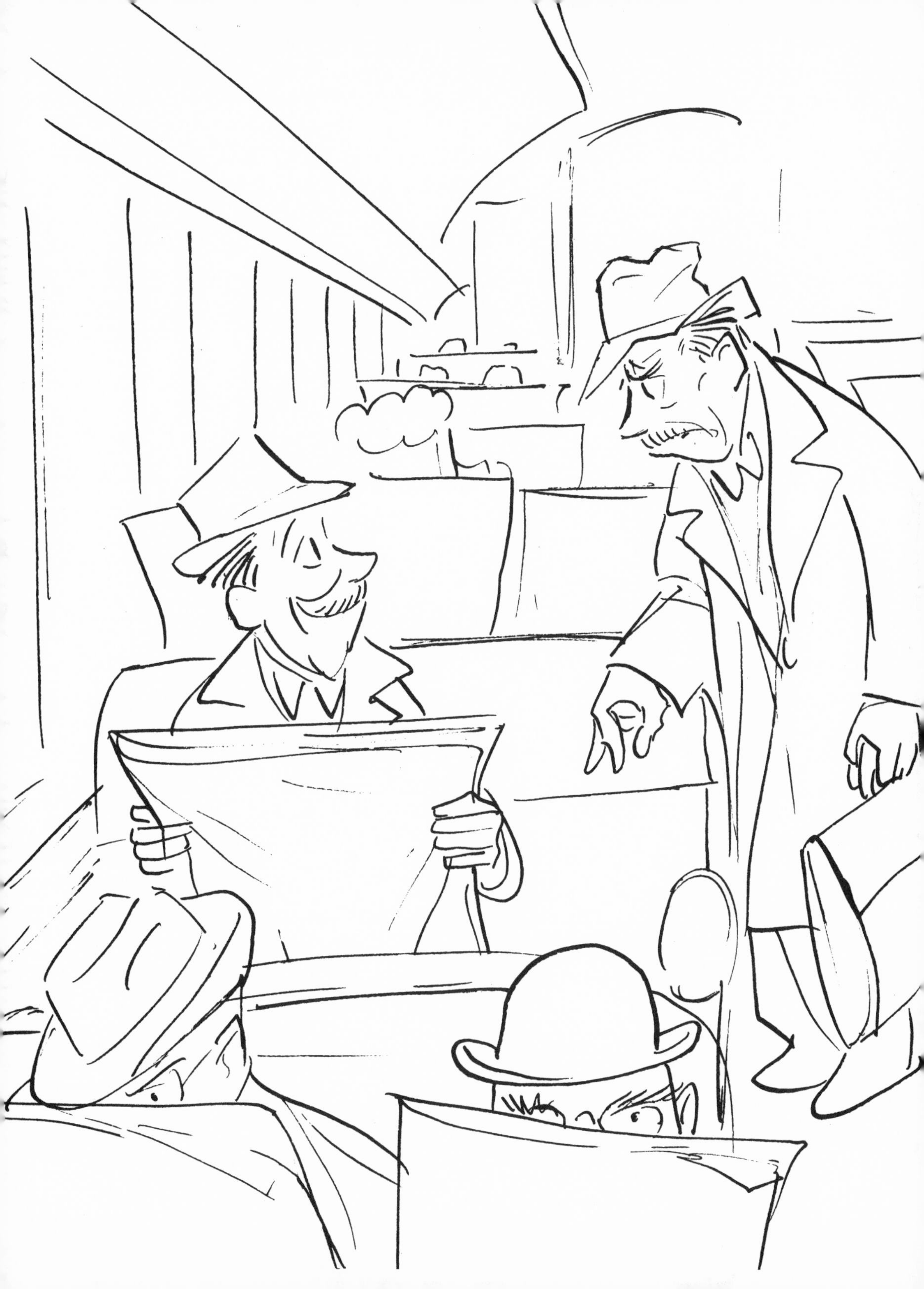

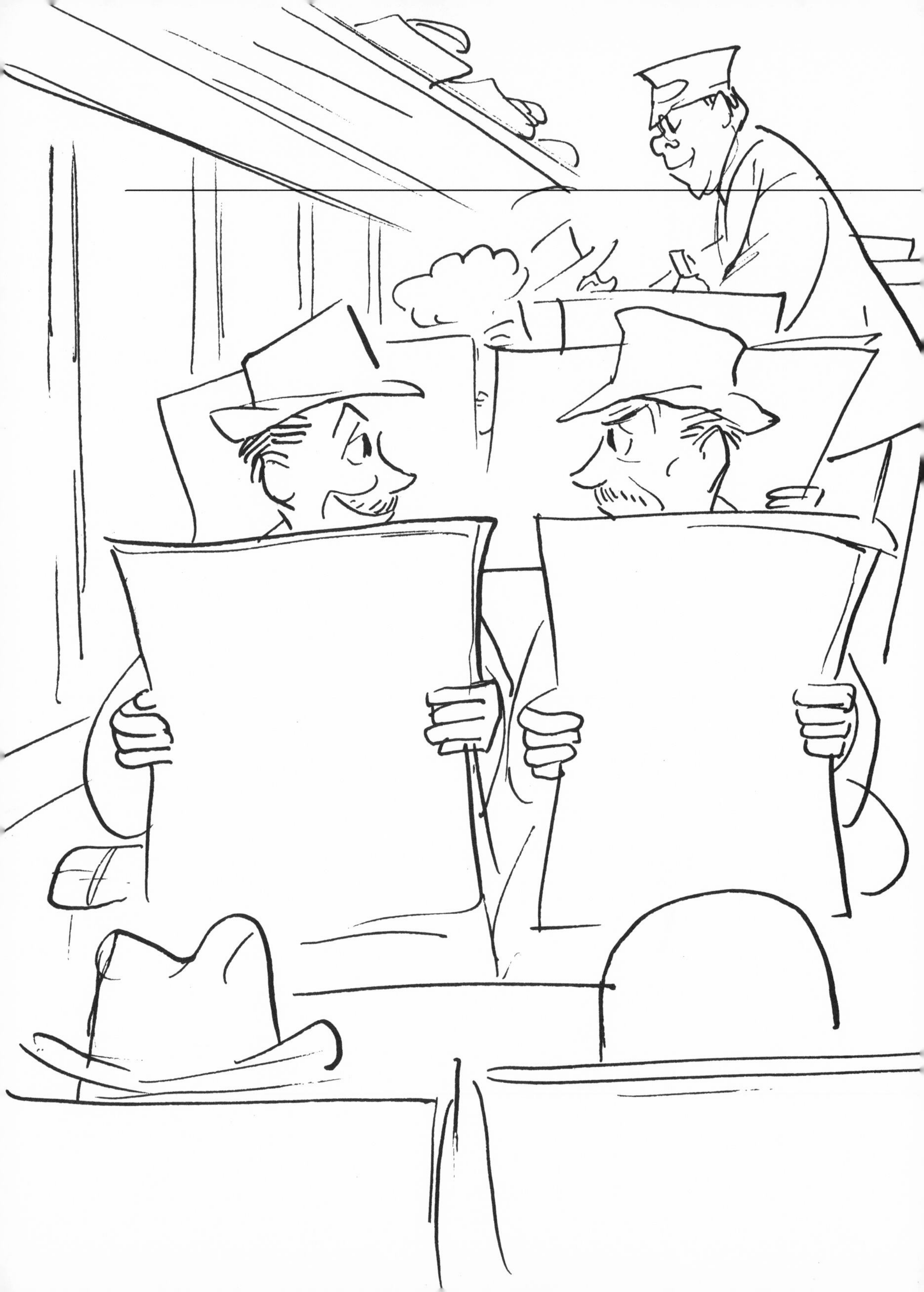

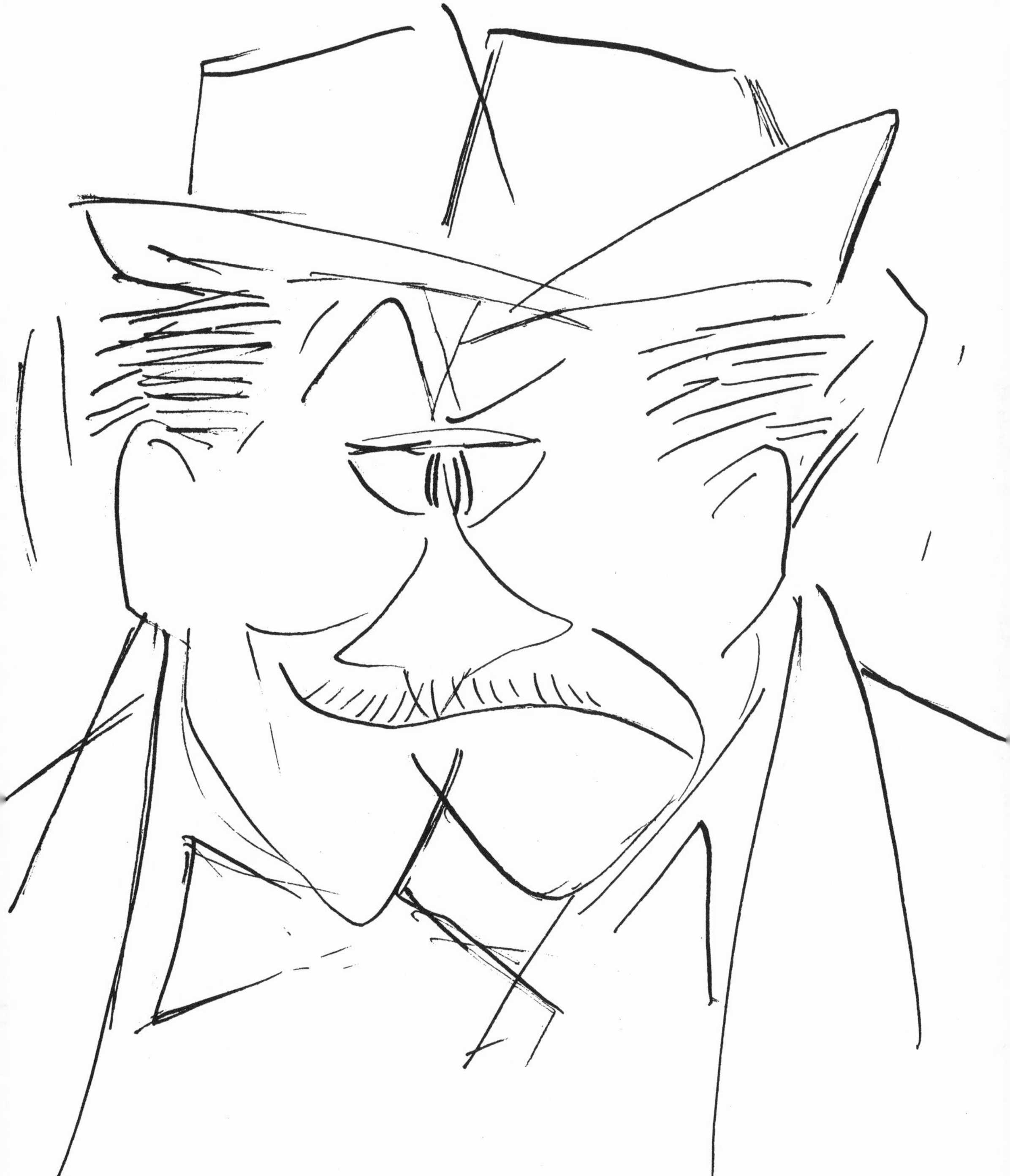

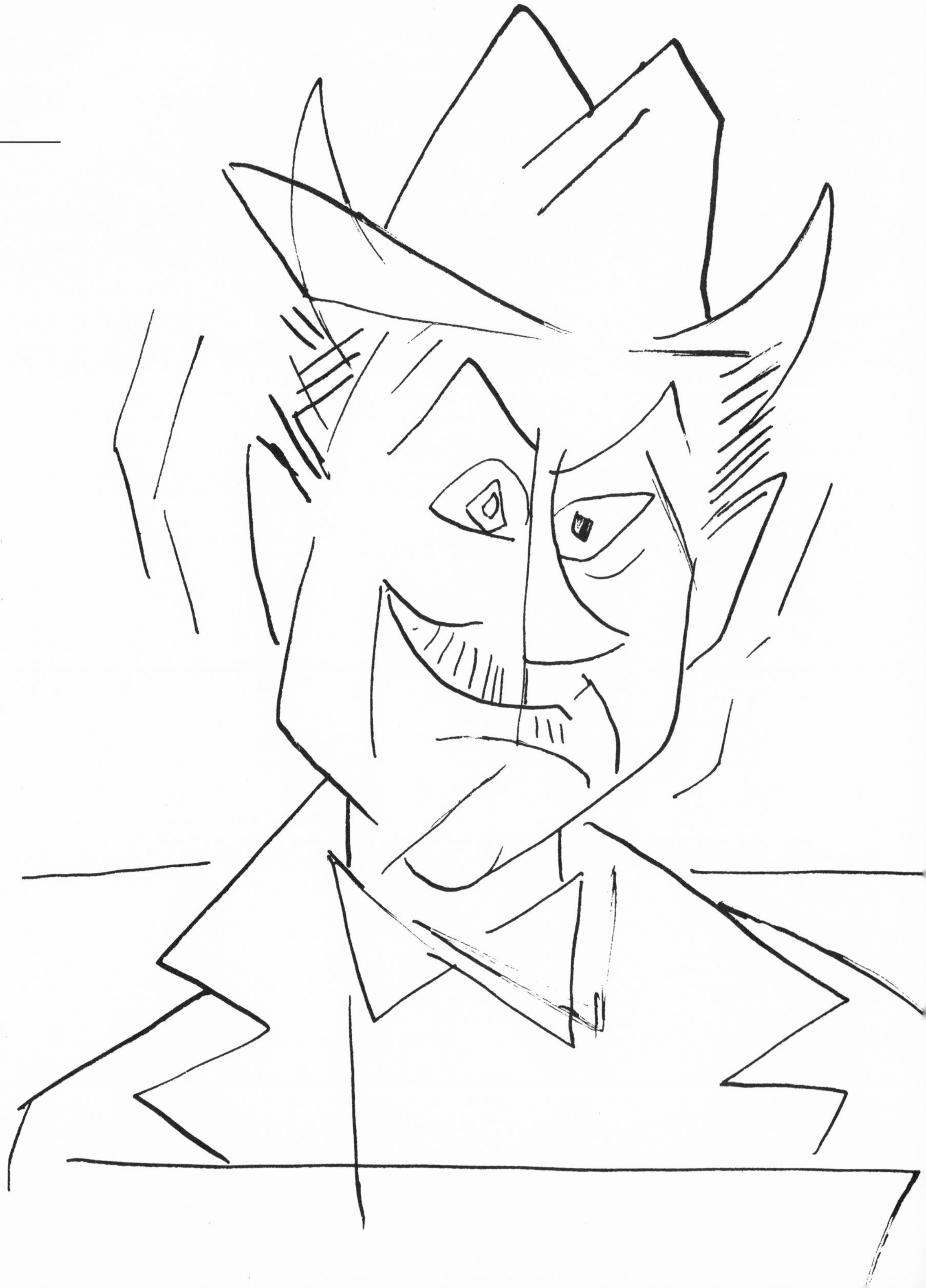

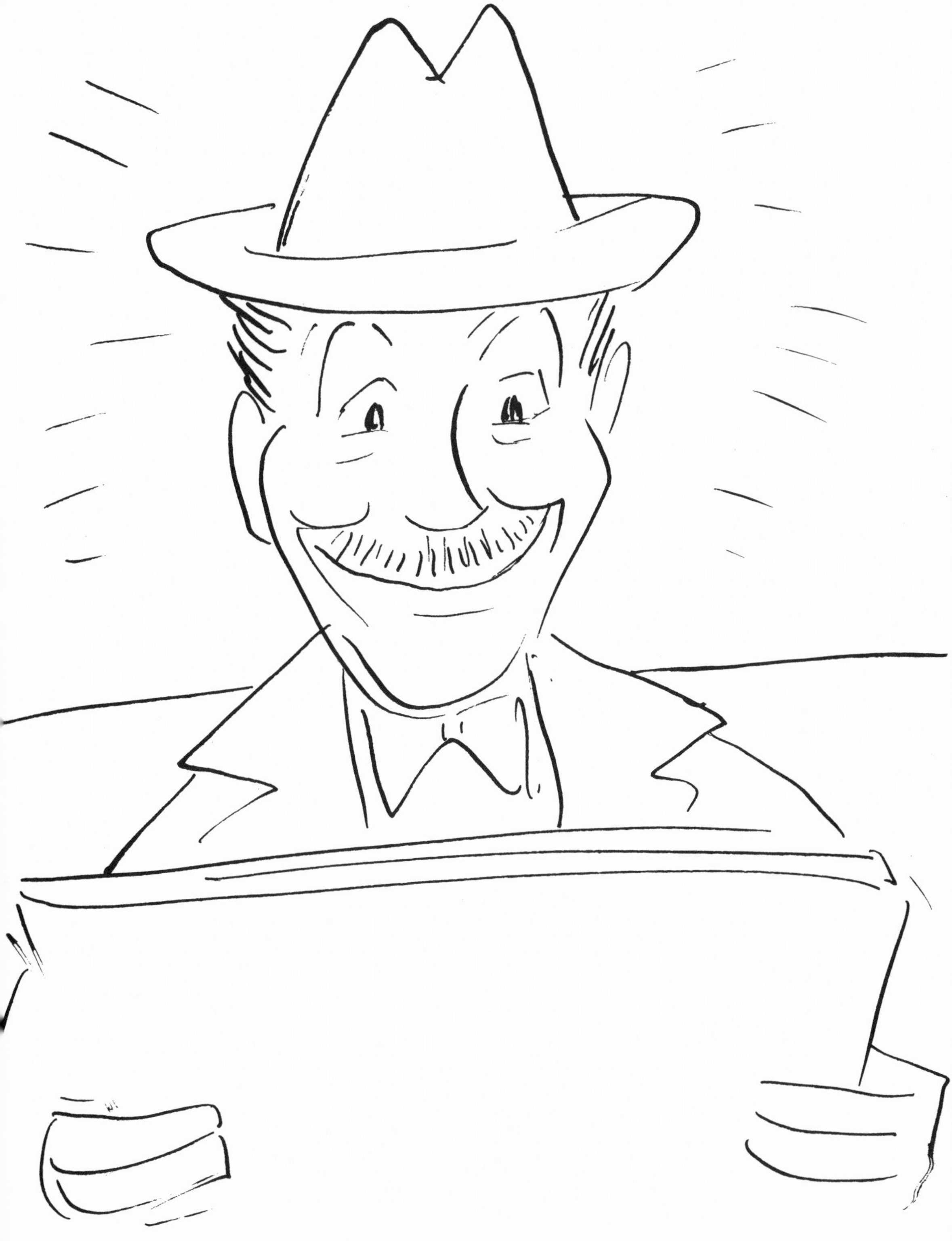

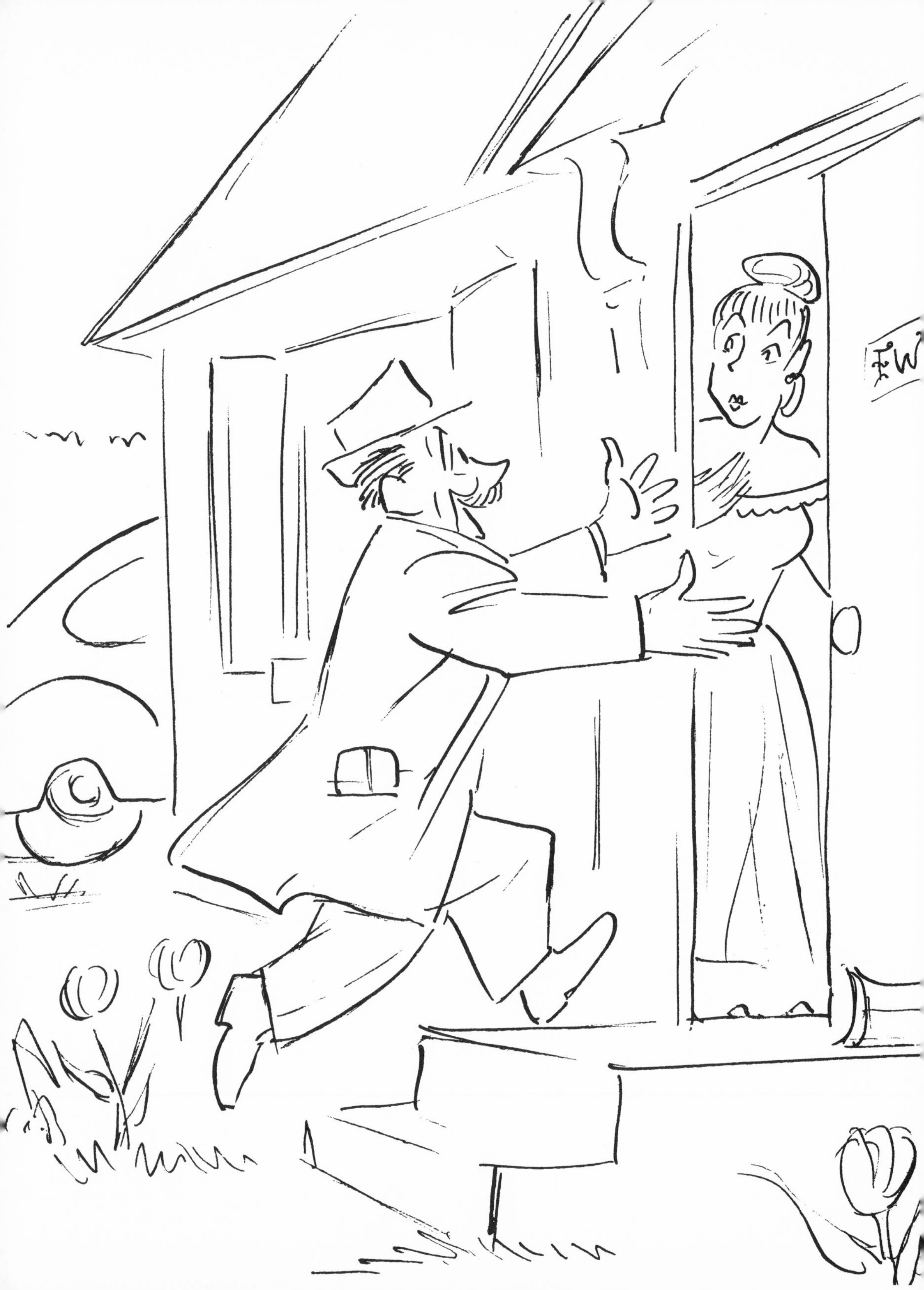

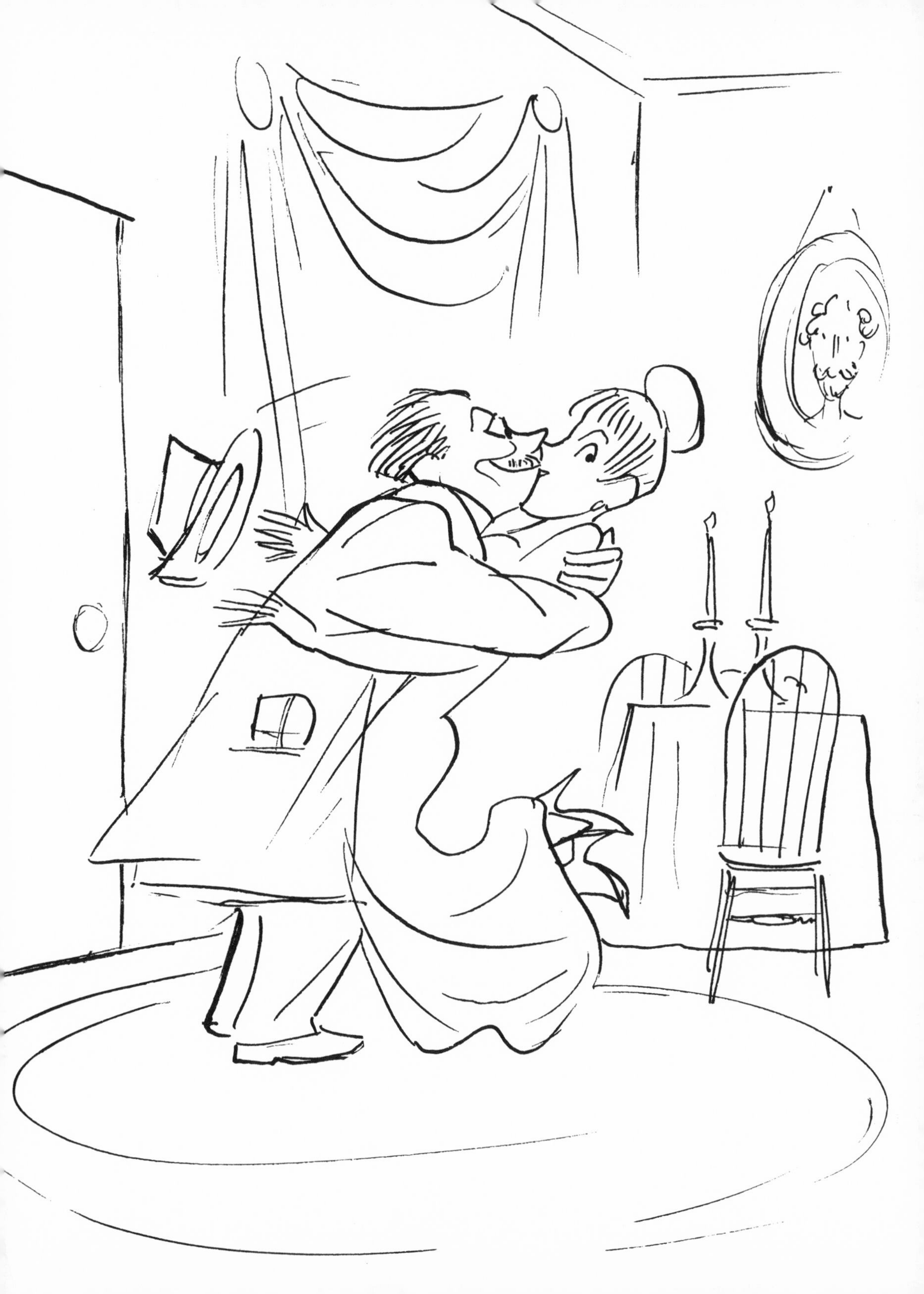

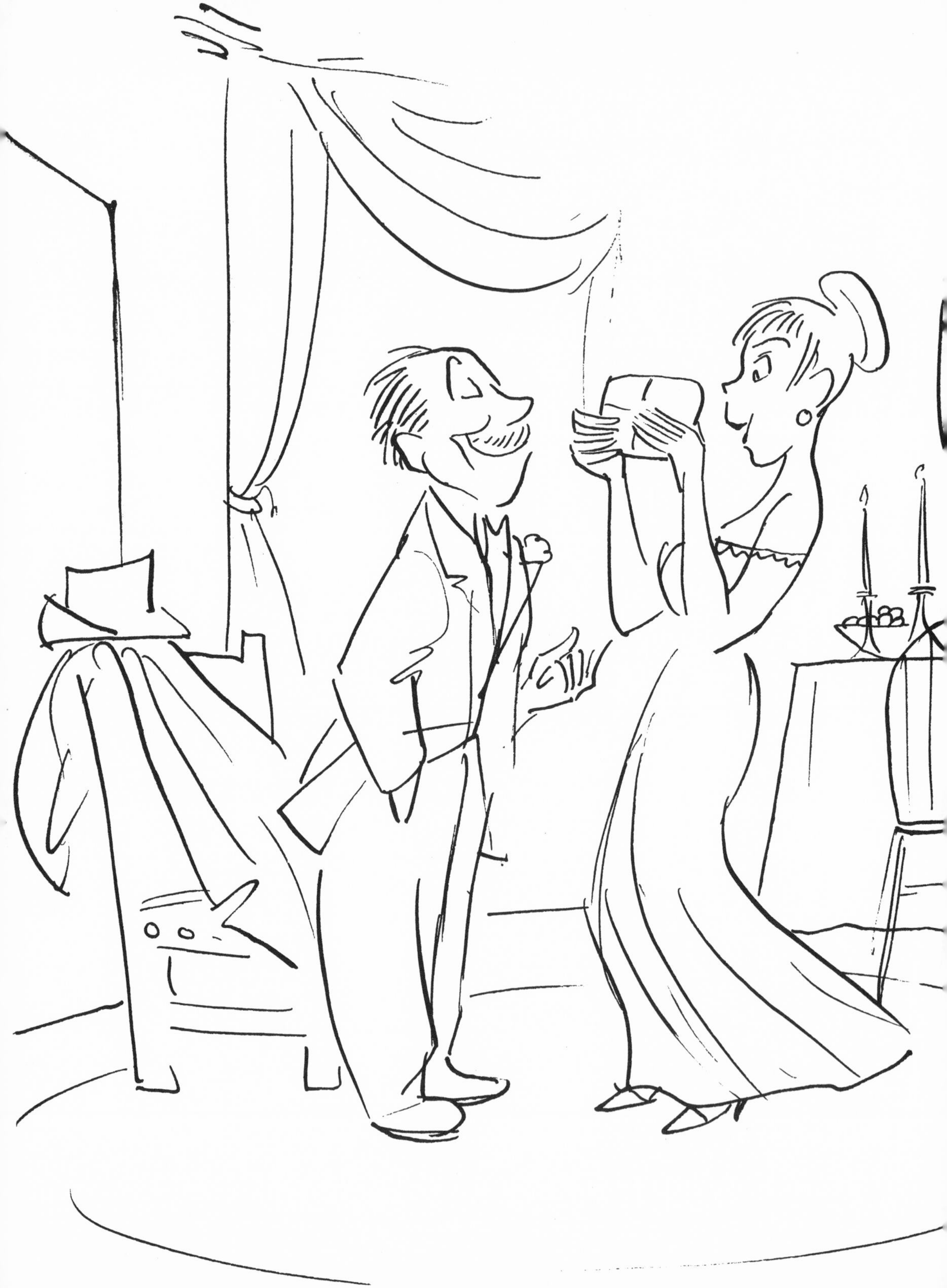

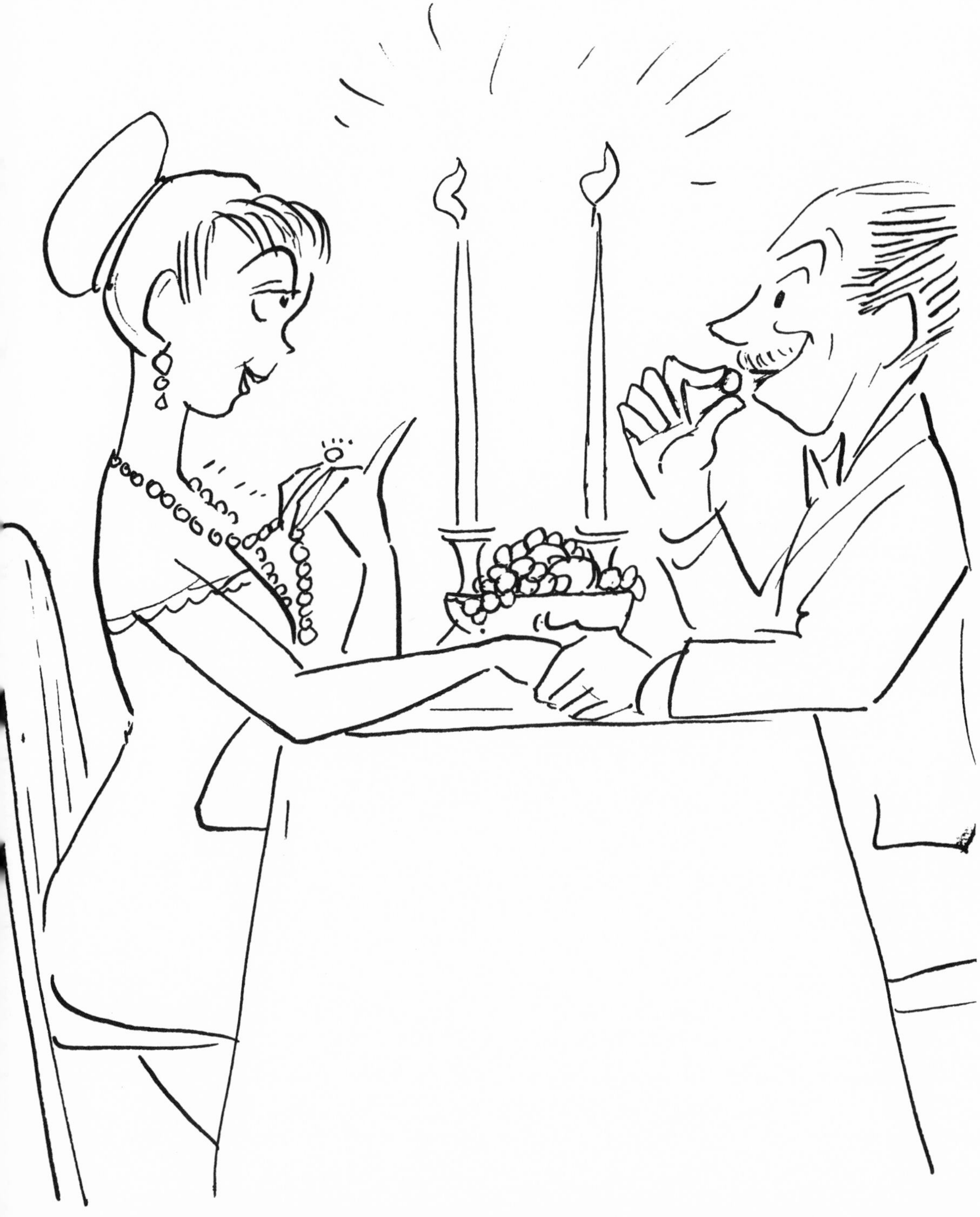

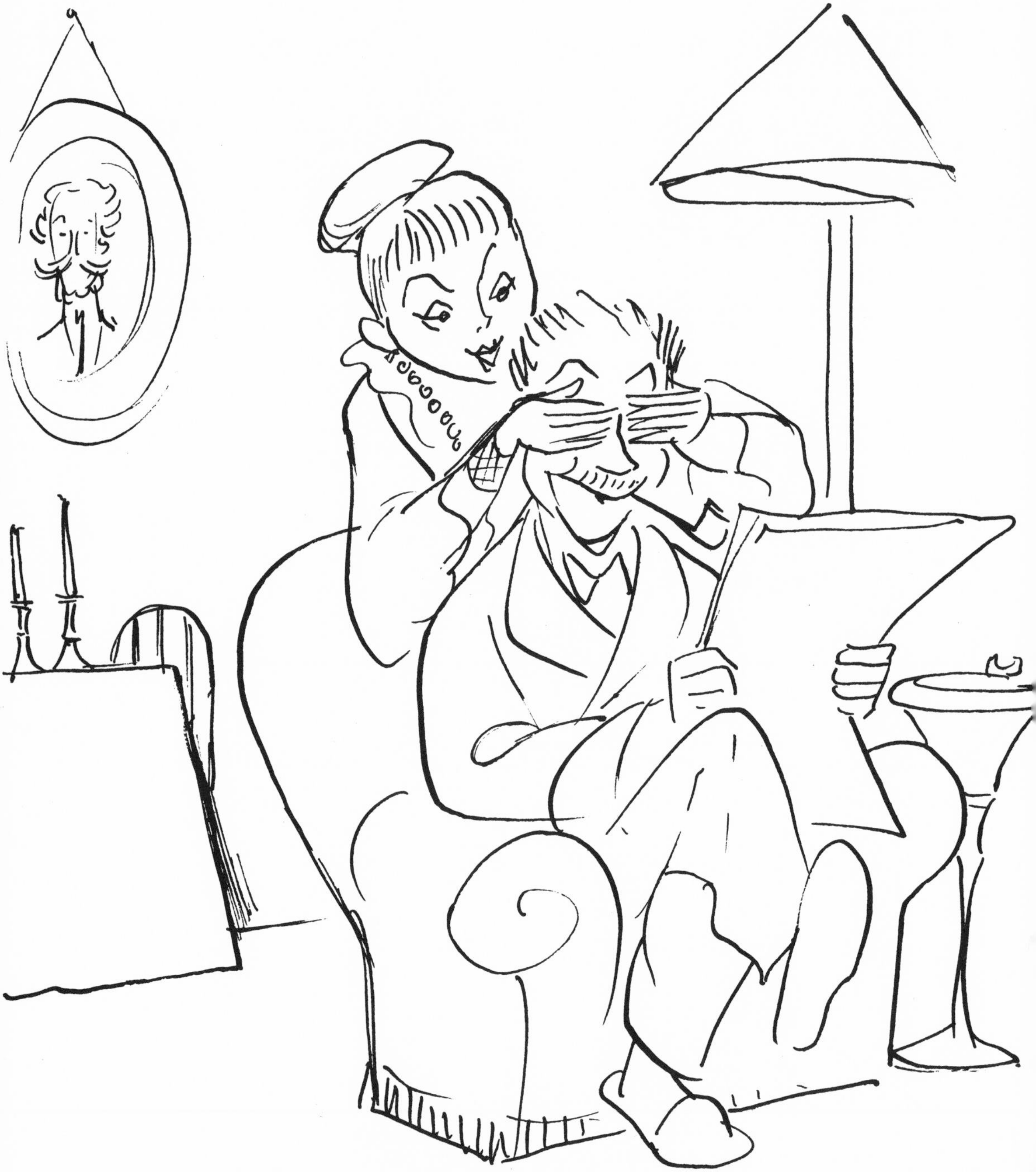

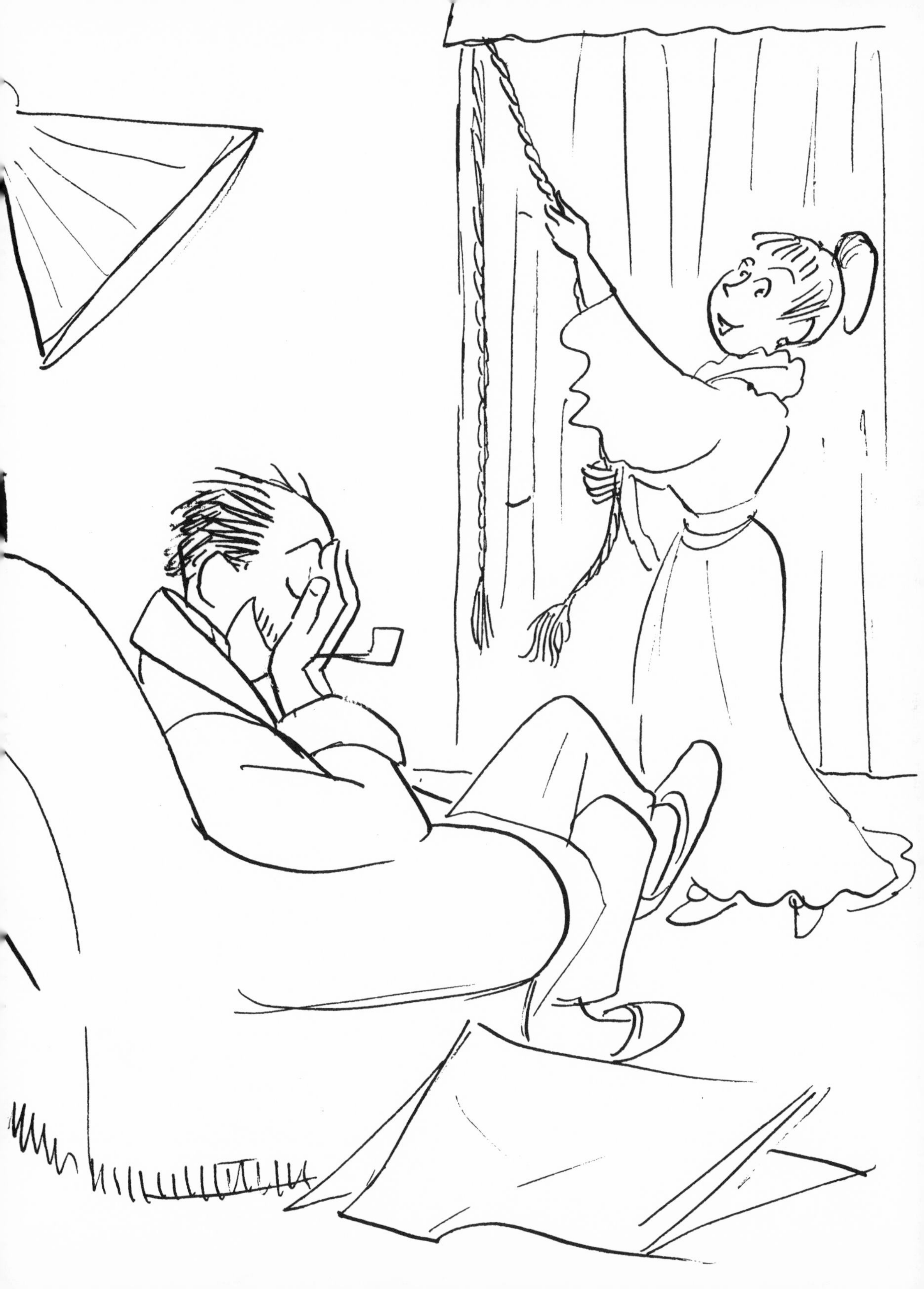

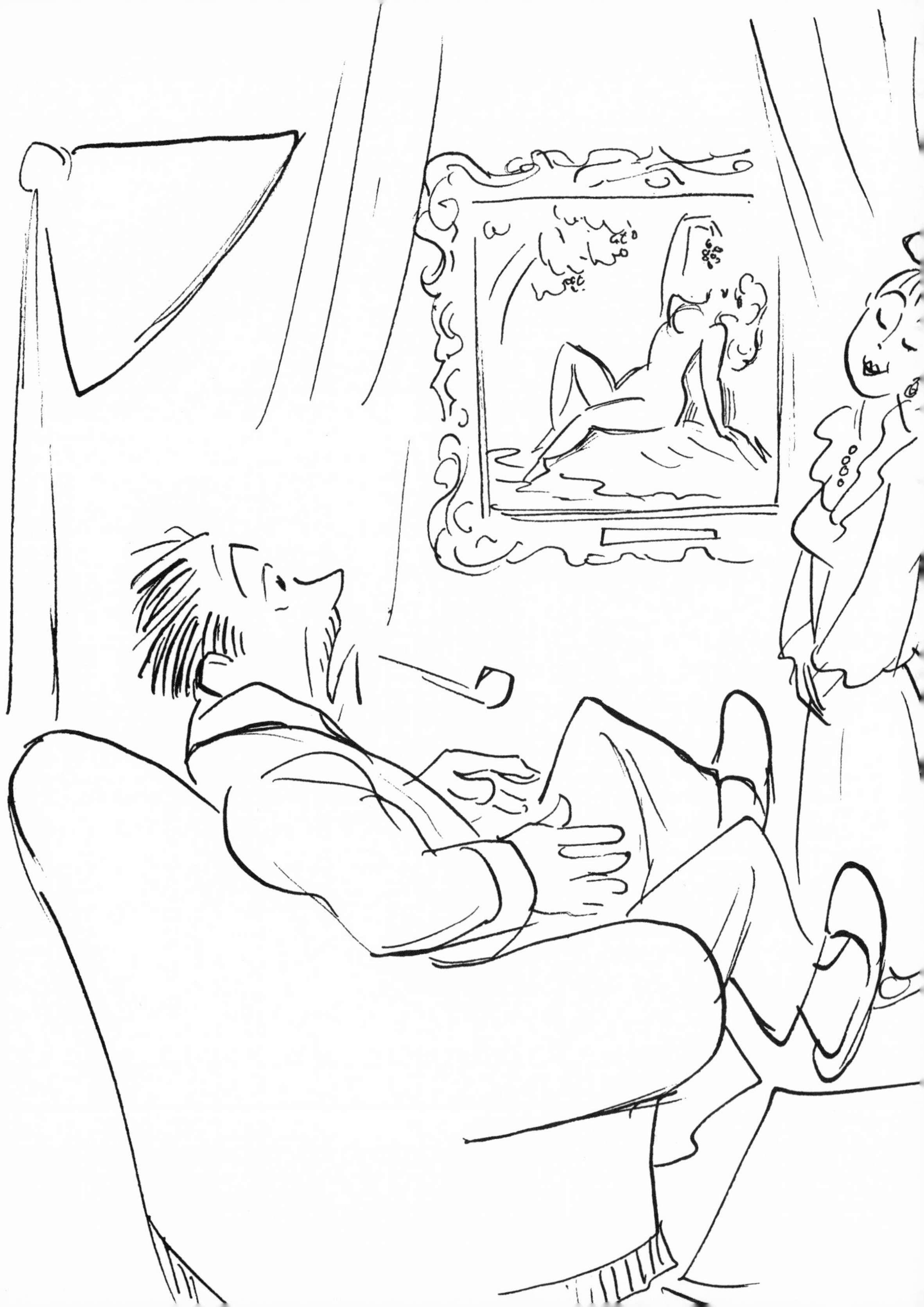

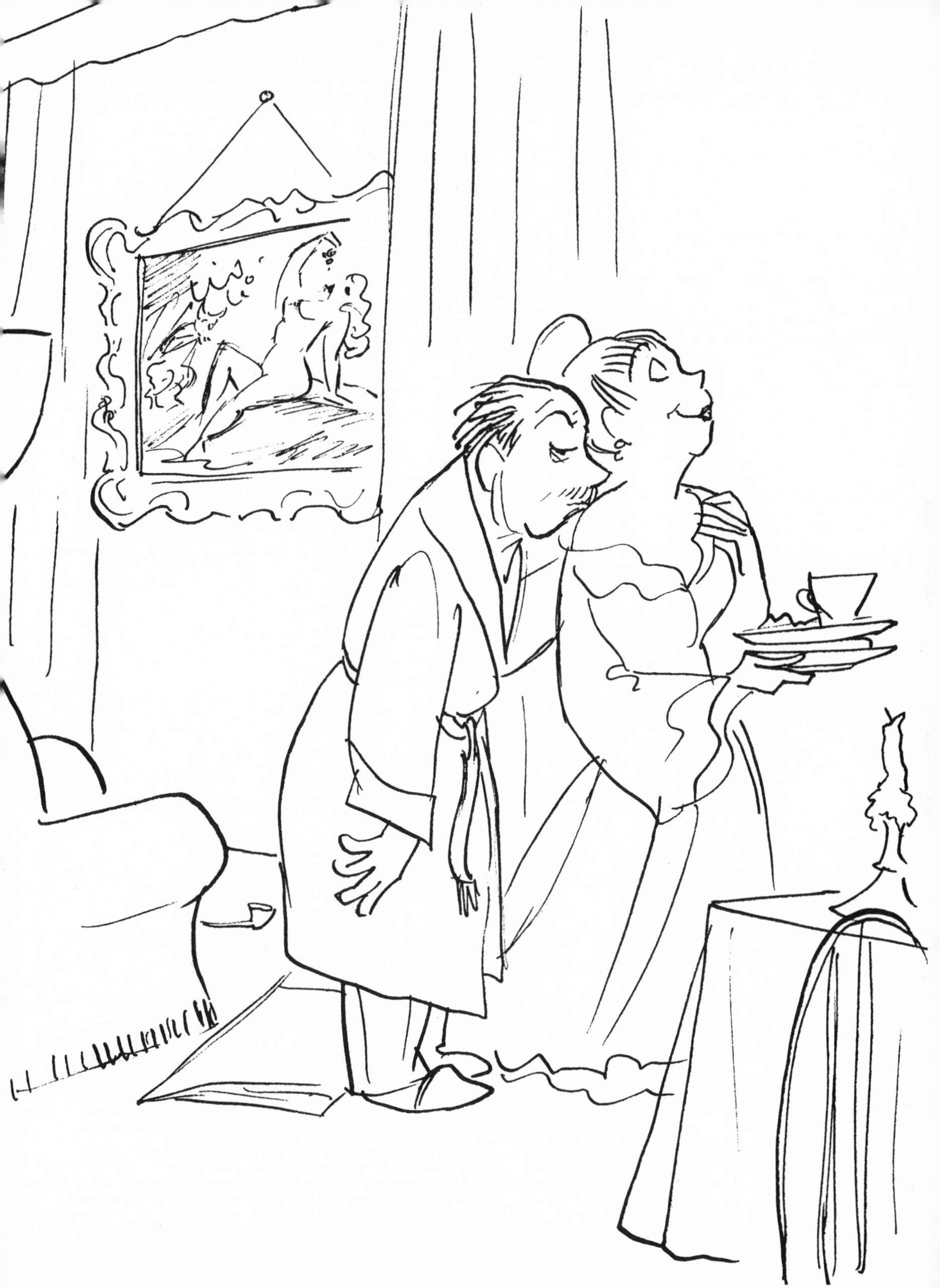

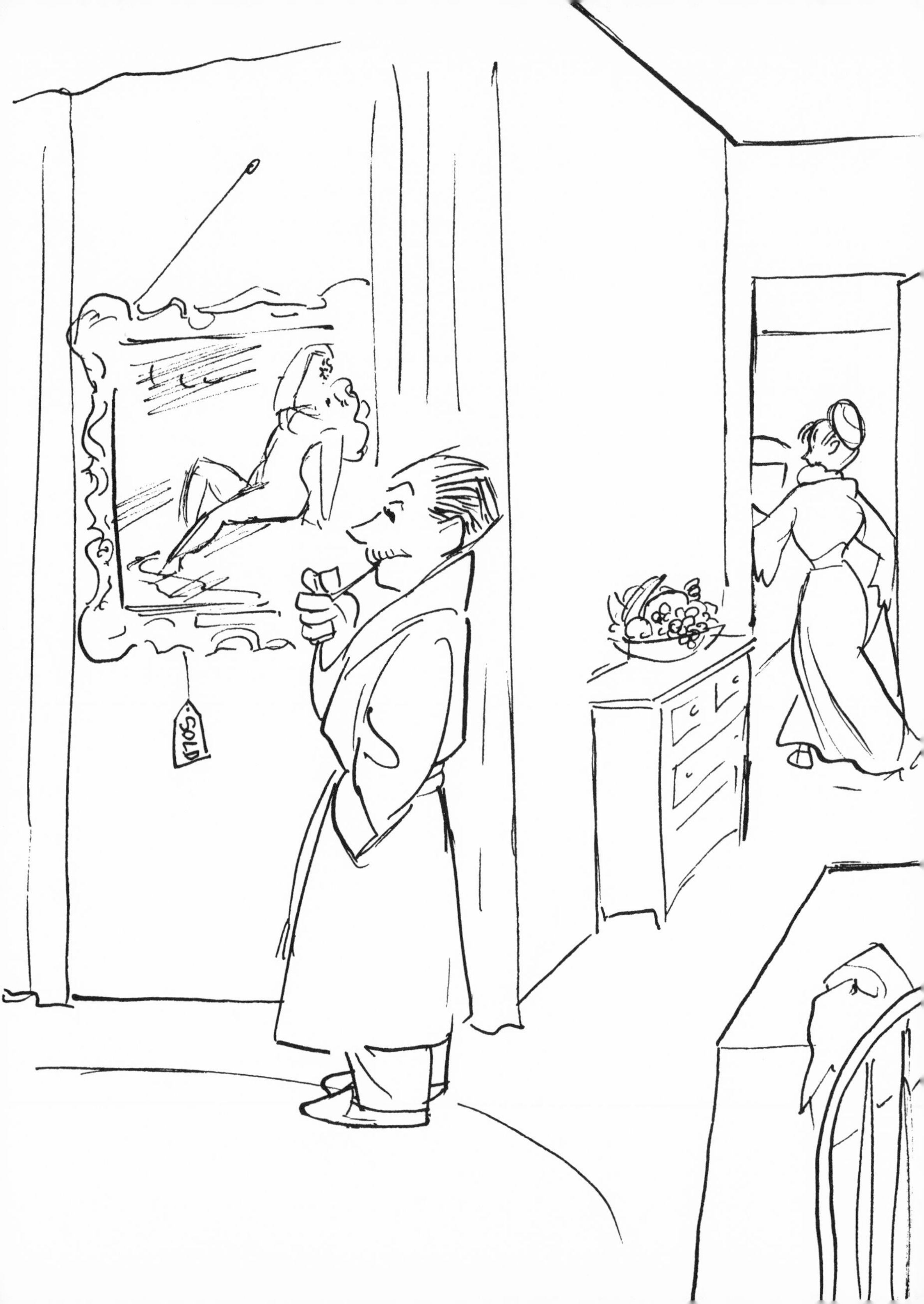
SOLD

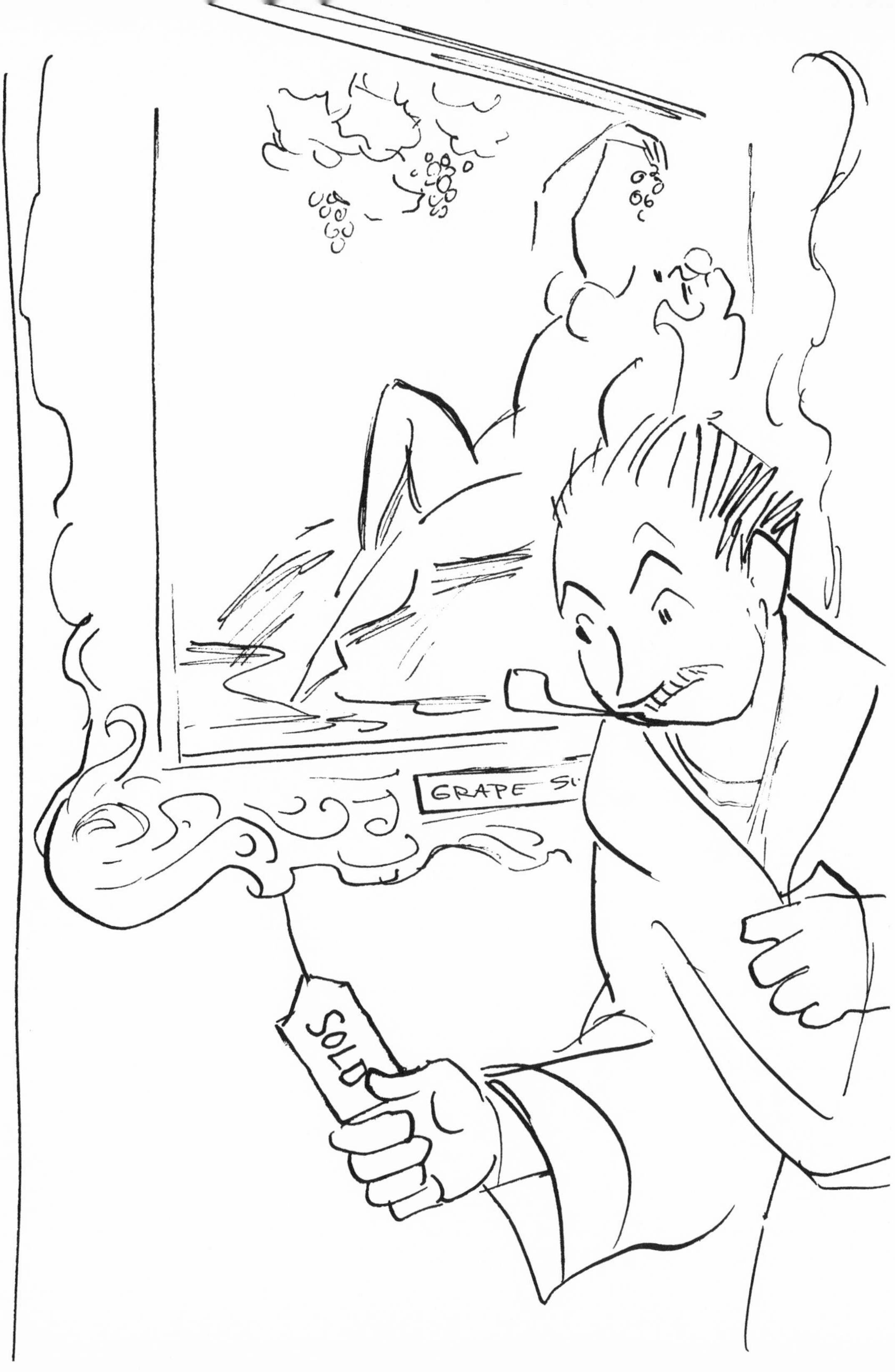
GRAPE
SOLD

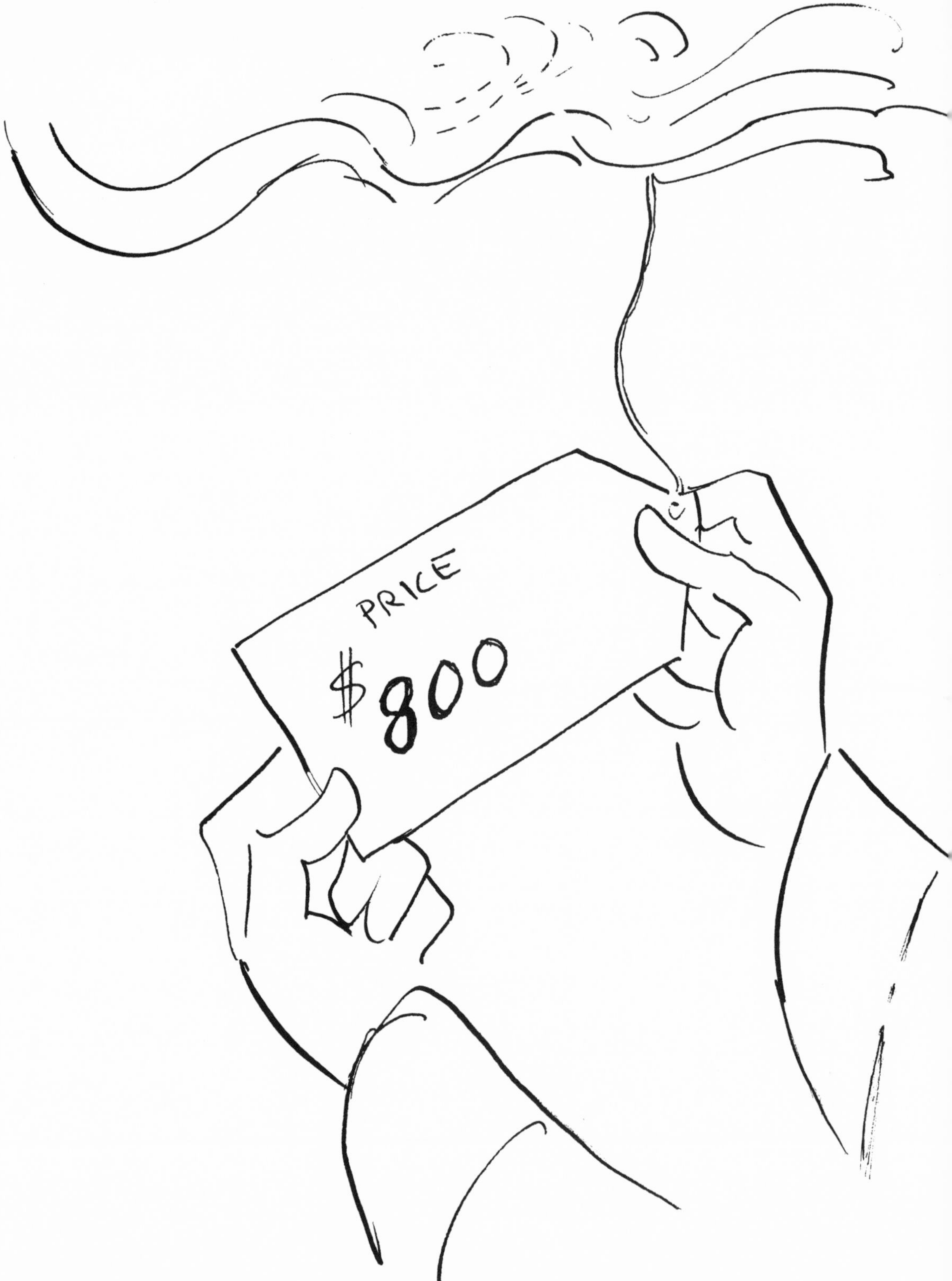
PRICE
$800

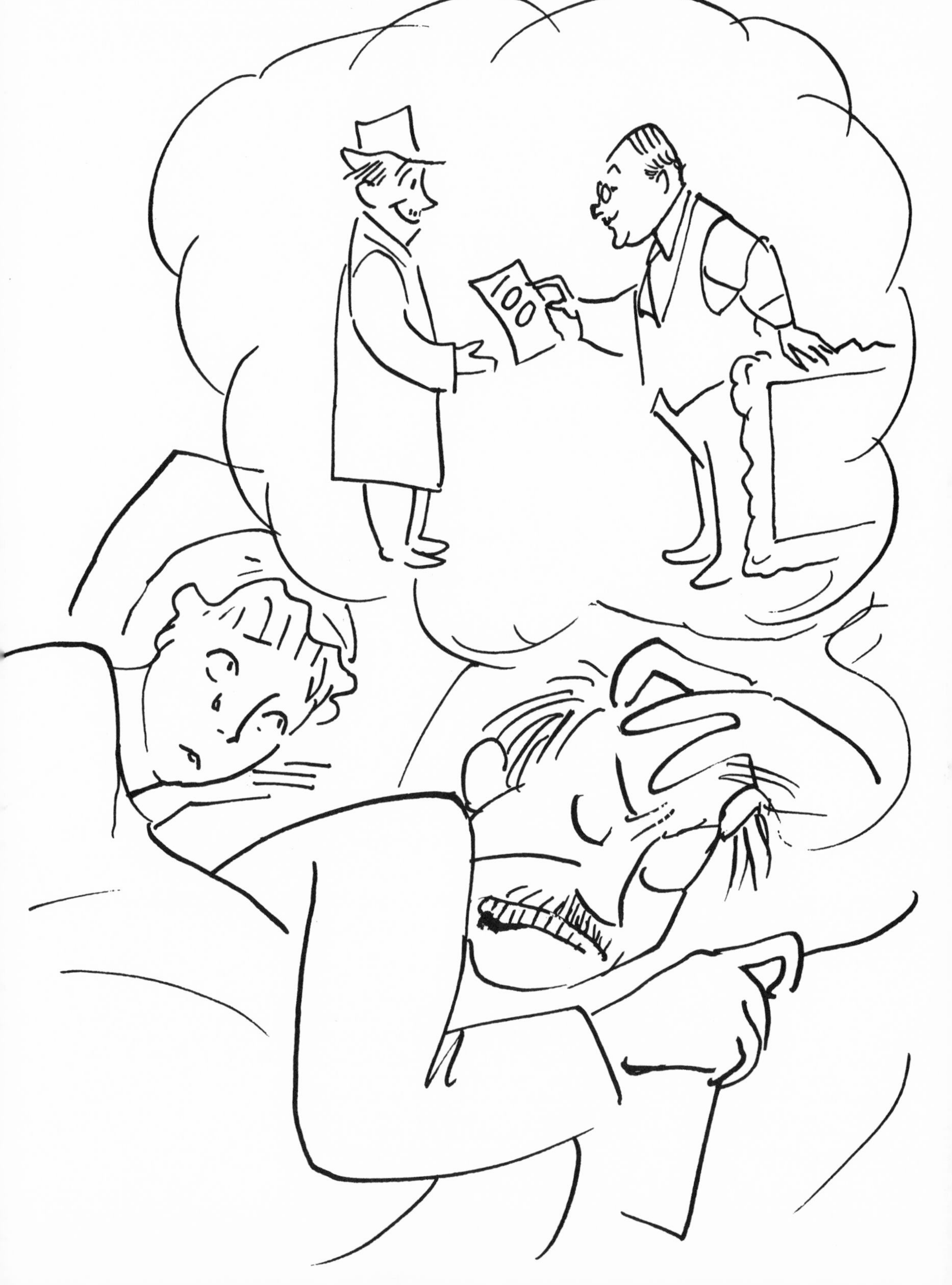
100

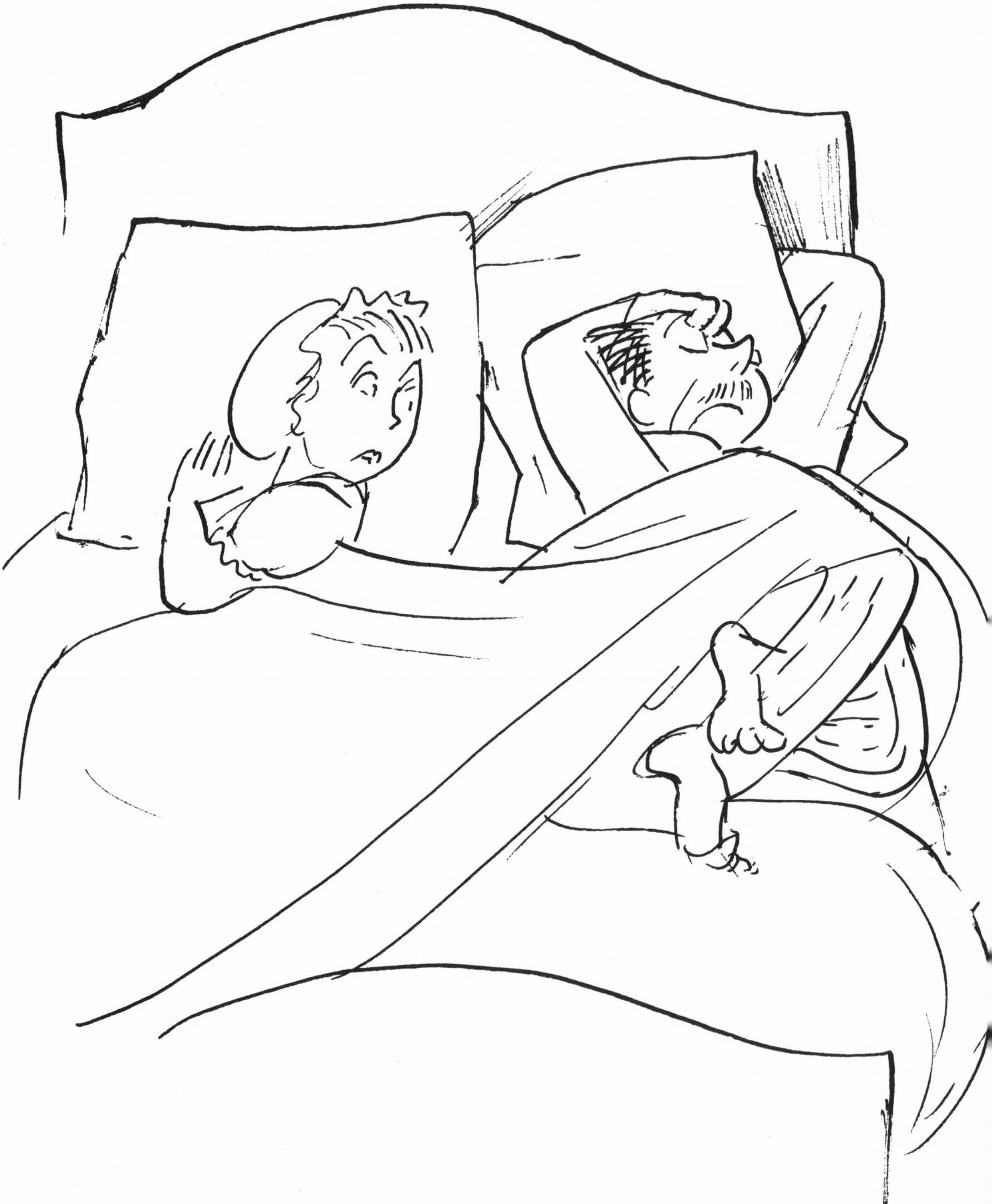

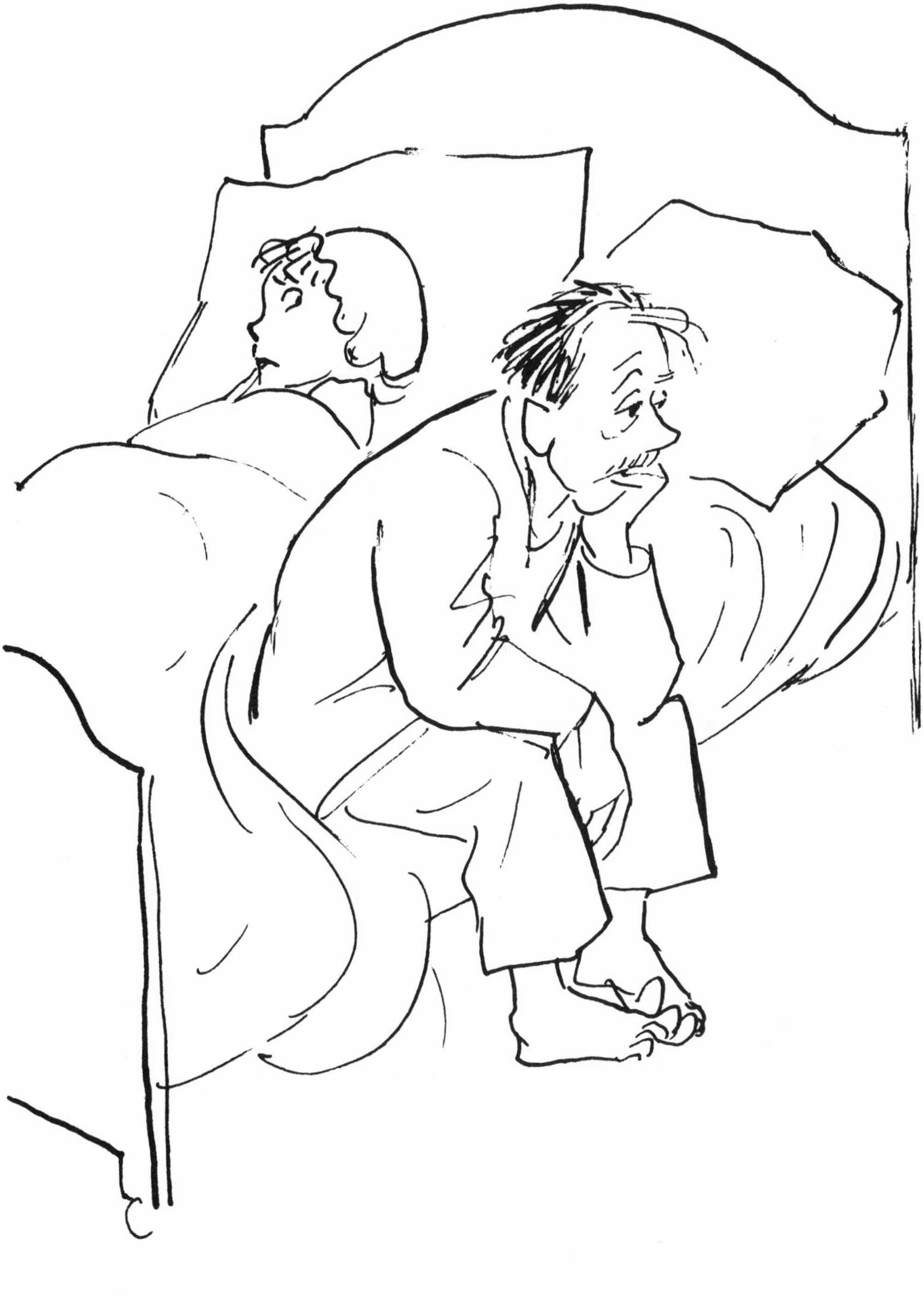

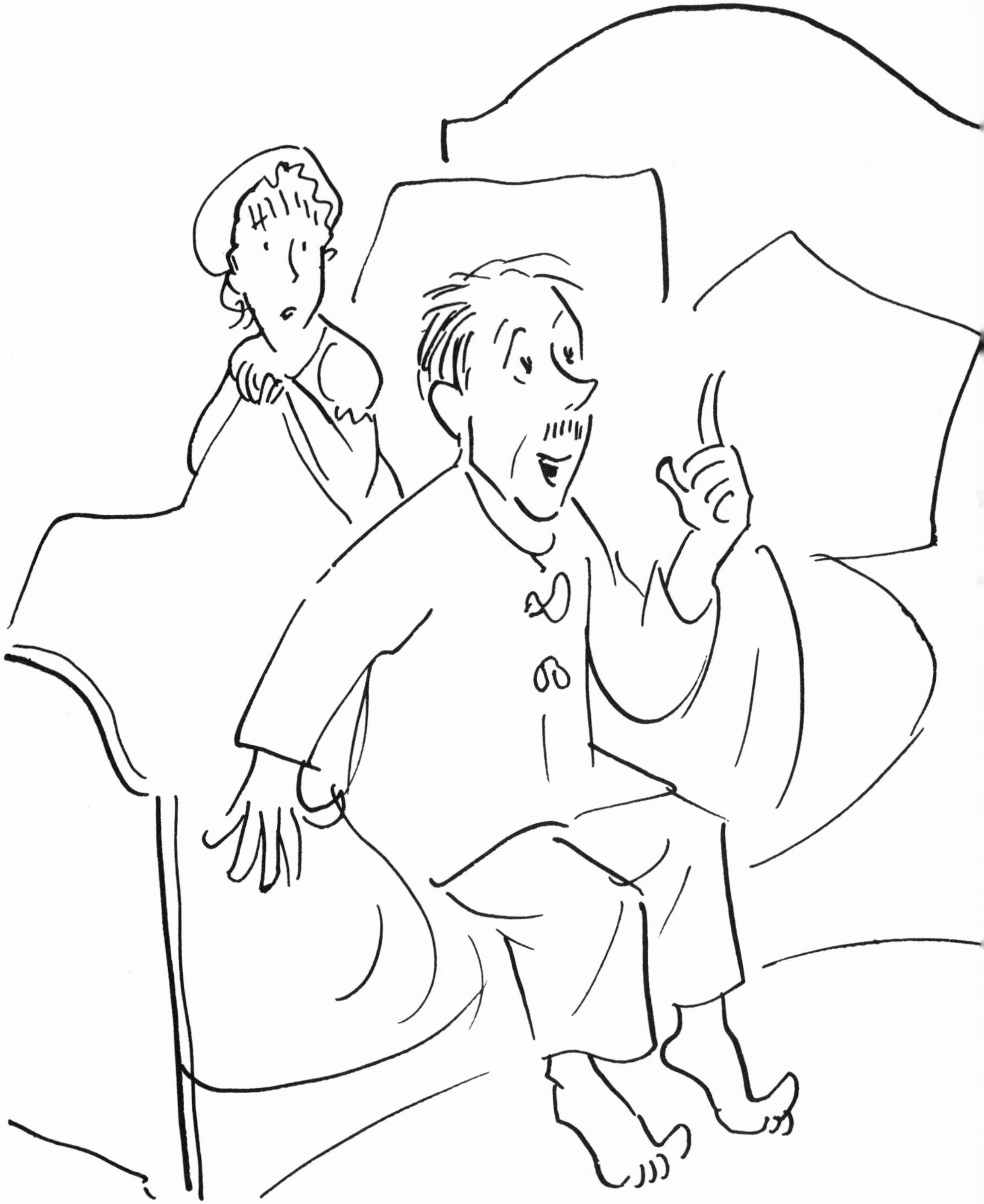

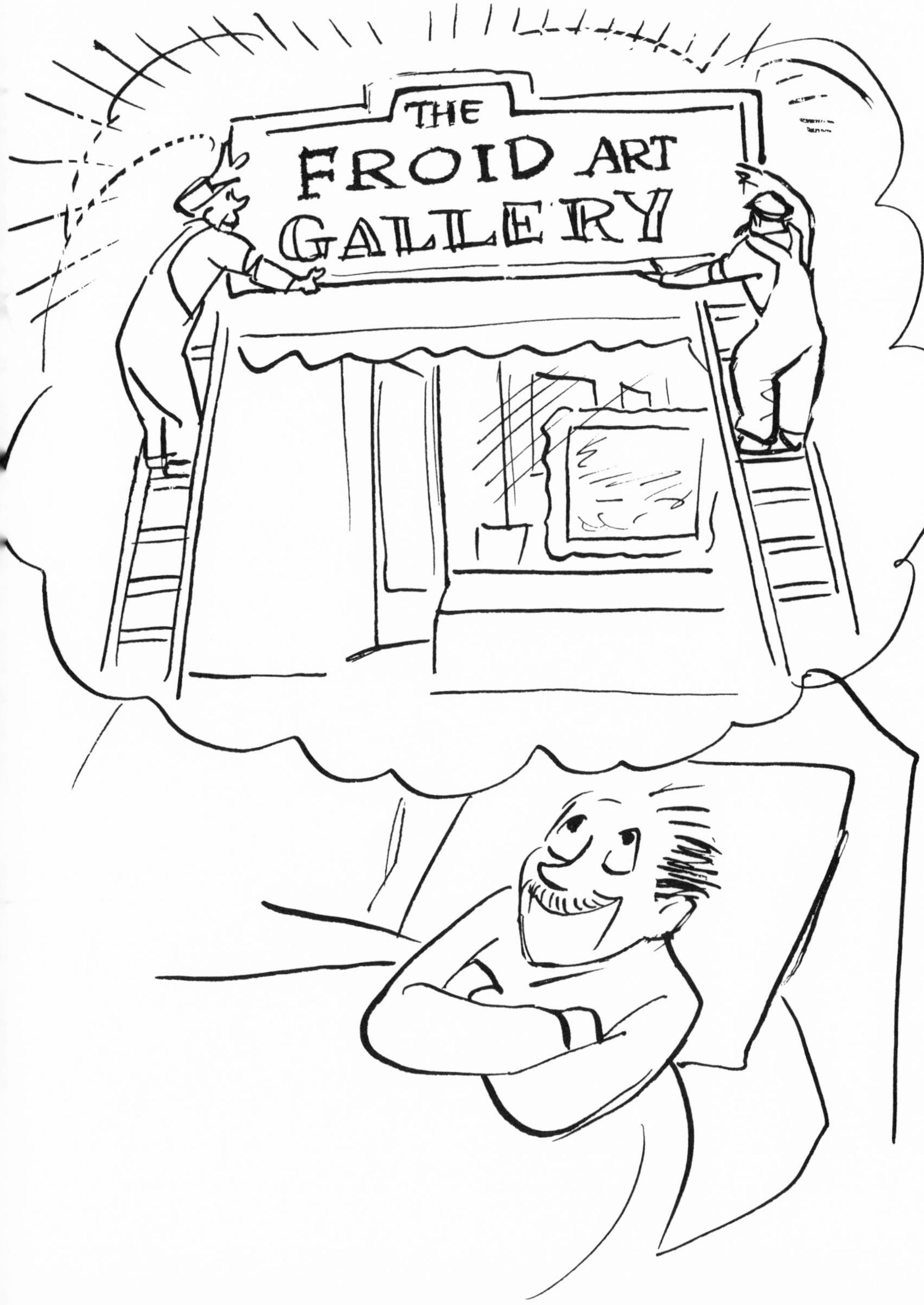
THE
FROID ART
GALLERY

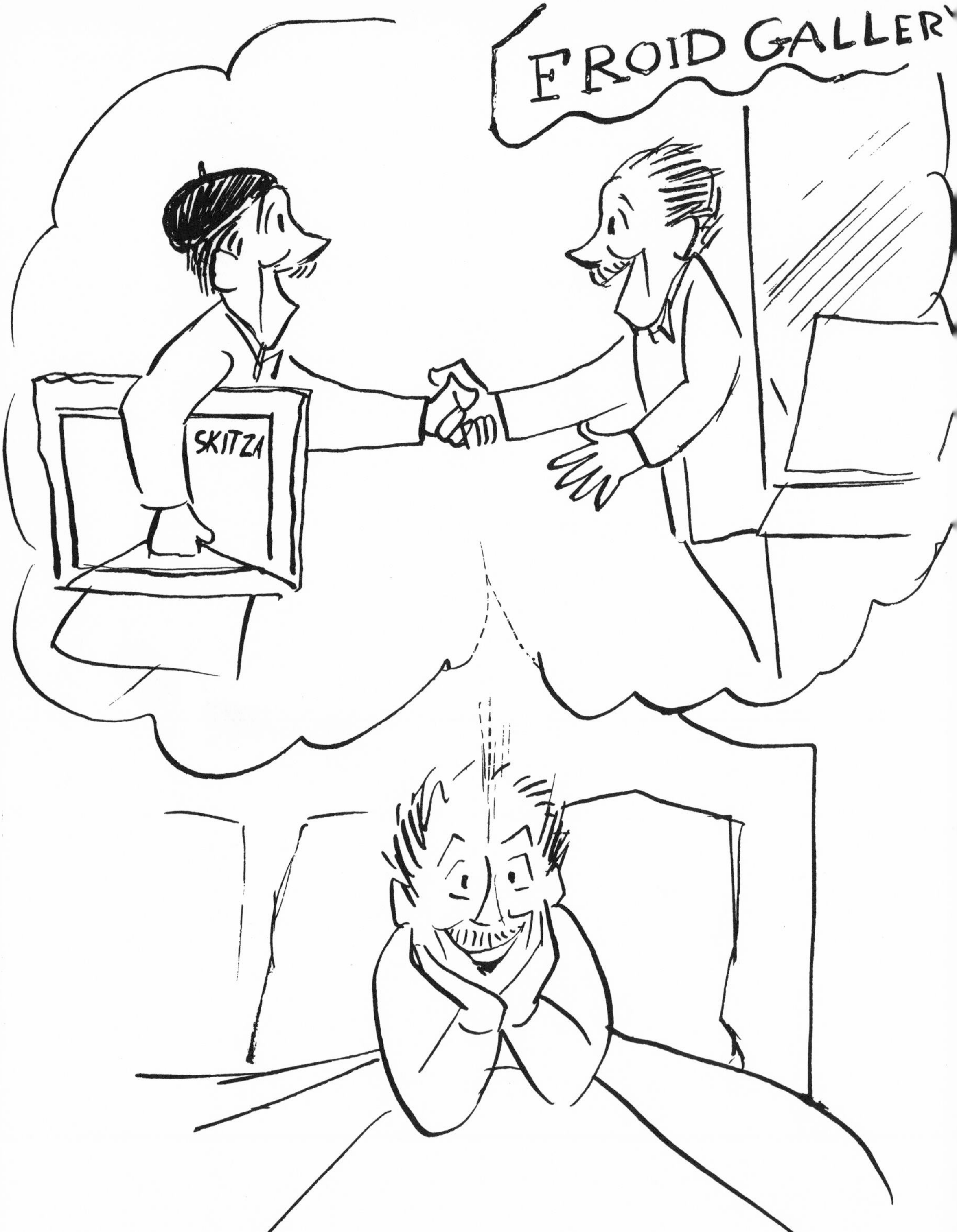
FROID GALLERY
SKITZA

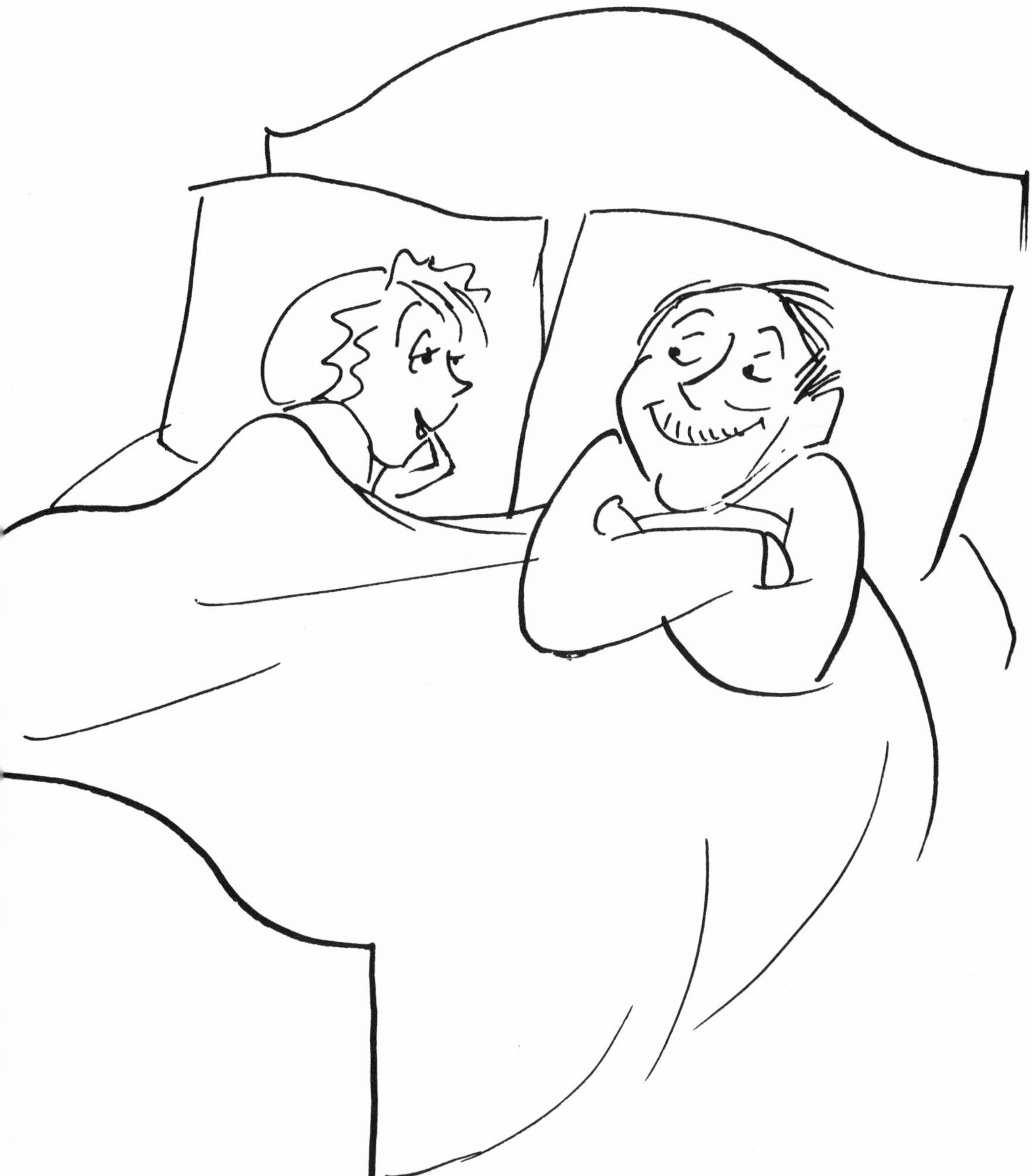

PUBLISHED BY DON FREEMAN
AT
JOHN D HOOPER LITHOGRAPHERS
343 FRONT ST.
SAN FRANCISCO, CALIF.

Skitzy: an afterword

The stage is set in San Diego. A pigeon is nesting in the letter B of an electric light sign atop a tall building, a theater. The bird leaves its nest, flying above the city. In the playhouse below, a spotlight shines on a young man, 21 years old, trumpet in hand. An artist who, since the age of five, has been making theatrical skits with his brother and the neighborhood kids in Chula Vista. It is time to leave the nest and find brighter lights. As he raises the trumpet to his lips, the auditorium fills with lively Depression-era jazz. These are rough times, the late 1920s, and the stock market is set to crash. Still, the talented and the restless shall prevail.

Don Freeman is a survivor. He makes it across the country on his musical talents. When he arrives in New York, he is set on becoming an artist. He loves this city: the energy of the street life and the theater empower his work. By night, his trumpet is his meal ticket. By day, his career is living, capturing life. He is out on the street with a sketchpad documenting what a photographer cannot. His pictures capture an energetic realism filtered through the eyes of a cartoonist. When he loses his trumpet on the subway one night, he comes to realize his focus—he will make a living with his drawings.

A cartoonist? It is easy to say this in retrospect, when Dr. Seuss and Jan and Stan Berenstain are household names. Don's work defies such labels. We can call him a classically trained artist as well as an illustrator and humorist. His work remains difficult to categorize, for it is both serious and cheerful.

If Don's life were a picture book, it would begin with a ringmaster's whip and a cheer from the crowd. Above all, he was an entertainer. His work unites an optimistic spirit with a grand theatrical sentiment. Like the title of his autobiography *Come One, Come All* suggests, his was a life worthy of many optimistic introductions and enthusiastic afterwords. This is definitely not the first time his work has been celebrated since his passing. In 1980, *The Day Is Waiting* was published – a story composed from preparatory sketches and watercolors for children's books. More recently, the 40th anniversary edition of his most beloved book, *Corduroy*, featured an afterword with Don's preliminaries, as well as correspondence with his editor.

Skitzy was created after Don embarked on his third career, writing books for children. Self-published in 1955, it ties together Don's humorous storytelling skills with keen observations of street life, the latter well-documented in his magazine *Newsstand*. At this time, Don had been a New Yorker for nearly 25 years. Quick at sketching from life, Don also had the patience to transfer these pencil drawings to stones and plates. A master lithographer with an outstanding sense of color design, Freeman created thousands of prints during his early years in New York and *Newsstand* was a chance for him to collect and distribute this work. While he painted as well, Don had a stronger interest in art that was reproducible. Using these media, he could sell and distribute the work himself without the constraints or pretensions of a gallery.

While *Newsstand* documented life on the streets of New York City, the public was more familiar with another aspect of Don's work: the theater. As a regular contributor to the drama pages of both the *New York Times* and the *Herald Tribune*, Don's theatrical drawings, as wide as the stage, stretched across three columns of text. Here, the drab and often somber sketches of the poor were replaced by images of beautiful showgirls, spectacular costumes, and fantastic backdrops. The strength of these theatrical drawings was demonstrated in Freeman's ability to depict the players, and perhaps, more importantly, his depiction of the stage itself. His pictures gave viewers something they couldn't get even if they attended the show: a backstage perspective.

For a long time, much of Don's life revolved around the theater, and the works he created convey the suspense and old-time presentation of this insider's world. The first book to use the stage setting that would make Freeman's work unique was *Pet of the Met* (1953). The story takes place on the set of a concert at the Metropolitan Opera House. In it, Freeman focuses on the goings-on backstage, although we also get glimpses of the concert itself and the audience's reaction. The techniques used in *Pet of the Met* would later be reworked in the even more effective *Norman the Doorman* (1959), the second of his books to make use of wide, stage-like pages and a backstage perspective. Freeman often revisited both this theme and format throughout his career, most notably with *Hattie, the Backstage Bat* (1970). This book, while not as well-known as others, is an amazingly perceptive parable of an outsider's view on the joys of the theatrical life.

In terms of style, Don did not follow trends. His drawings always remained loose and without borders. Sometimes he worked in watercolor, and other times in charcoal or scratchboard. While his work was often whimsical, the settings were usually realistic. He pushed the limits of children's books by being one of the first artists to create effective African-American characters and stories where humor was as important as the moral. In 1954, he created *Beady Bear* in a bold, black and white scratchboard style. The style and theme in this book share many similarities with the book that would become *Corduroy*. *Corduroy*'s success is in part due to the combination of the *Beady Bear* style with Freeman's more theatrical settings. Where *Beady Bear* differs is that the story features a journey out—a toy bear learns from a book that there is a world outside of the boy's house in which he lives. He sets out to find a cave and make new discoveries.

This journey out, away from the staged set, must have been on Don's mind at the time. As he moved away from the theatrical world, and began to focus more on children's books, his characters also began to escape the familiar. In *Mike's House* (1954), a book illustrated by Freeman, a young boy loses his way en route to the library and discovers a new adult world of policemen and waitresses. Similarly, in *Mop Top* (1955), a boy embarks on a journey about town to get a haircut only to have some strange encounters with his neighbors before returning home. An even greater escape fantasy, however, comes from this very book, a much more personal story for Don.

While *Skitzy* is by no means a children's story, it shares the sophistication and diligent execution of the above-mentioned works. What it lacks in finished style and color, it makes up for in the spontaneity and the confidence of its execution. It differs from the picture books in another key way—rather than relying on text, it's a mostly wordless story. In order to compensate for the lack of descriptive text, Freeman used more pictures. This deliberately gives the book less of a staged look and imbues it with more action than any of Freeman's works before or after. In fact, many of the sequences in *Skitzy* have an almost animated style, which is quite different from his picture books.

Ten years before *Skitzy*, Freeman illustrated James Thurber's *The White Deer*. Similar to Thurber's most famous work, *The Secret Life of Walter Mitty*, *Skitzy* presents, in a humorous manner, perspectives of a working class man's fantasies. Like Thurber's *The Unicorn In The Garden*, which was made into an animated cartoon in 1953, there is an emphasis on psychology and the tension between man and wife. Both works are unique attempts from the time period at bringing mature themes in a cartoon format to an adult audience. While *Skitzy* is not necessarily an autobiographical work, it would not be incorrect to view this as one of Don's most personal pieces. Unlike Thurber's *The Unicorn In the Garden* (which originally appeared in the *New Yorker*), *Skitzy* never really had an audience. It was a piece that Don published himself several years after he had wrapped up his work on *Newsstand*. If the character is meant to represent Don, the author of *Skitzy* is a separate persona from the children's book author. Here is an artist who went out on his own, created a questionable artwork that might not have an audience, and decided to sell it himself. It is a bold, brave work. Perhaps it was ahead of its time.

If this is Don's New York success story, the work still remains humble. His 1971 children's book, *Penguins of All People*, also featured a fantastical journey to New York. In this case, the father Penguin seeks success as an ambassador from Antarctica at the United Nations. When the penguin takes the stage, he amuses the crowd with his nervous antics. It is then that the simplest of intentions seems to be an answer to all of the world's problems—laughter. When the father returns home, he realizes that his son, whom he had originally ignored, provided him with this solution from the beginning. Therefore, in Don's more realistic journey out and return home, it is no coincidence that he continued to explore these themes in children's books. His picture books, while hugely successful, still remain personal and honest. Probably the best evidence of this is that his son Roy, is the namesake of his other most well-remembered creation, *Corduroy*.

Since Don Freeman's death in 1978, several of his unpublished books have been given a new life through posthumous printings including *Gregory's Shadow* and *Earl the Squirrel*. Even if you are familiar with all of Don's 32 picture books, *Skitzy* still has plenty of surprises to offer. I am thrilled that after more than fifty years, this work will now be rediscovered by new audiences. There's even a happy ending; Don wouldn't have had it any other way.

—Dave Kiersh, September 2008